SOCIALIST ALTERNATIVE

This work was published by Red Flag Books, an imprint of Socialist Alternative, Australia's largest revolutionary Marxist group.

Find out more about SA, read our fortnightly newspaper and browse the bookstore at *redflag.org.au*

How Workers Took Power

The 1917 Russian Revolution

SANDRA BLOODWORTH

© Sandra Bloodworth

First published in 2008

This edition published by Red Flag Books
Melbourne, June 2023

ISBN 978-1-922927-04-0

Red Flag Books is an imprint of Socialist Alternative
redflag.org.au

Subediting and proofing
Tess Lee Ack

Layout and production
Oscar Sterner

Cover
Oscar Sterner

Printed by IngramSpark

Contents

	Preface	11
	Introduction	17
1.	The February Revolution	21
2.	The impact of the February Revolution	31
3.	February: the unfinished revolution	39
4.	The struggle for October	47
5.	October: the workers take power	69
6.	The Bolsheviks and the masses	81
7.	After October	93
8.	The first step in the international socialist revolution	99
9.	Was there a more peaceful, parliamentary alternative?	115
10.	The relevance of 1917 for today	129
	Gender, class and the Bolsheviks	135
	Glossary	161
	Notes	165

For **Zain**, **Jonas** and **Shan**,
the youngest people I spend time with.

With their unflagging enthusiasm for everything around them, they are a constant reminder that there is no better way to spend one's life than in the struggle for a better world for the children of today – for socialism.

Acknowledgements

In our society individuals are regarded as virtually autonomous beings because capitalism emphasises competition and so collectivity is derided. However, no book is the product of an isolated individual. And this is even more the case in the socialist movement. The ideas of Marxism have to repeatedly critique and compete with the dominant ideas that justify capitalism. So this book is a product of decades of political discussion and developing theory drawing on the experiences of workers' struggles. So I pay due tribute to all those who have struggled to maintain the ideas of revolutionary Marxism through thick and thin. In particular I acknowledge the collective contribution of members of Socialist Alternative, through informal discussions, debates, their writings and political activism to this book which will bear my name as the author. Specifically I want to thank Diane Fieldes, Corey Oakley and Mick Armstrong who gave comments on earlier drafts which significantly improved it and to Tess Lee Ack for editing the final text.

Sandra Bloodworth, February 2008

Million footed: a body. The pavement cracks.
A million mass: one heart, one will, one tread!
Keeping step! Keeping step!
On they march. On they march.
March, march...
Out of the factory quarters, smoke-wreathed,
Out of the black dungeons, filthy rat holes,
He came – his finger bent like pincers,
Burst the thousand-year-old chains rattling about him –
Came now the new ruler of the street,
Like flecks of blood
Crimson flags waved above him. Steel hard fists
Are raised aloft. The bones of the bourgeoisie whine.
But he speaks:
"All this is mine!
"Streets, palaces, canals, the Exchange, the Bank,
Arcades, granaries, gold, materials, food and drink,
Libraries, theatres, museums,
Pleasure grounds, boulevards, gardens and avenues,
Marble and splendour of bronze,
The poet's poem and the singer's song,
Towers, ships, cathedrals, space all round,
All this is mine!"
The houses thunder back. The highway clamours,
The giant stands fast

– Demyan Bedny, 1917

Preface

THE RUSSIAN REVOLUTION OF 1917 brought an end to the bloody slaughter of World War I and inspired millions around the globe to strive for a better world. In Germany, workers talked of "learning Russian" when discussing what to do about the war in 1918.

The Russian Revolution has much to teach us. It is imperative that we listen and learn the right lessons. We should not be surprised that this momentous period in history is the subject of vigorous debates – because if the correct lessons are promoted, capitalists will not feel so secure in their neoliberal world. They would prefer the book was closed on the issues arising from this revolution. And it is not surprising that many historians give us either partial or inadequate accounts. This is true of all history. It is just that this one is of such world-shattering importance.

Marxism can bring to light the best understanding because it begins with class, not just the class on whose side we stand, but with the *struggle* between the opposing sides. The genuine Marxist traditions provide us with the theoretical method to trace the relationship between objective circumstances and the conscious intervention of individuals, organisations and the mass of people. Marx argued that humans make their own history, but in circumstances not of their own choosing. And as humans act, so they change their consciousness. We will witness this process in all its drama between the months of February and October. Workers, soldiers and peasants respond to the situation, learn lessons through a combination of their own experience and political arguments made by the various organisations, and respond, determining the course of history.[1]

Tragically, for nearly six decades of the twentieth century the authoritarian state that emerged from the ruins of the Russian

Revolution claimed the mantle of "Communism", distorting the language, the content, and the spirit of Marxism. The world was mostly divided into two camps. There were those who said this showed that socialism was only a dream, and if workers misguidedly overthrew the existing order they would create a monster worse than the one overthrown. And there were those who cheered on the repression and brutality of the Stalinist state. Both positions strengthened the position of the rulers both East and West.

Then in 1989, the Stalinist bloc began its collapse, and millions paid for the horrors of not communism, but state capitalism. Like all capitalist societies, it suffered the inevitable crisis, this one on the scale of the Great Depression that had devastated the rest of the world in the 1930s. Now, even many of those who had saluted the Stalinist monolith switched sides and declared that socialism was dead. Of course, they got a huge welcome into the fold of those who had always argued that capitalism is the pinnacle of human achievement.

But throughout this sorry epic, there was a tiny minority who refused to call Stalin's counter-revolution a step towards socialism. First there was Trotsky and his supporters who suffered vilification, exile and even death in order to keep alive the ideas of genuine Marxism. After World War II Stalin, with the connivance of Roosevelt and Churchill in the West, sent the Communist tanks careering around Eastern Europe to create new supposedly Communist states at the point of a gun. The Trotskyists were thrown into disarray. It was one thing to call Russia a "degenerated workers' state" as Trotsky had. It was entirely another to accept that these new states in which there had not been workers' revolutions, could be "workers' states".[2]

And so Trotsky's baton passed to Tony Cliff, a Jewish Trotskyist from Palestine, who returned to the archives to try to understand the nature of this phenomenon that claimed, in defiance of every internationalist principle of Marxism, to be "socialism in one country". Cliff drew on the fundamentals of Marxism to explain that there was nothing intrinsic to the revolution that caused the rise of Stalin, as almost all historians of every persuasion contended.[3]

Marx had argued sixty years before the revolution that without the material basis to provide for everyone, socialism was not possible, and that all the old muck of class society would revive if a revolution brought workers to power in a situation where this did not exist. That material base could only be established in Russia by help from a workers' state in the more advanced West.[4] The defeat of the revolutionary movements that swept Europe in the years immediately after 1917, not events inside Russia, sealed the fate of the workers' state.

Cliff documented in great detail how every vestige of workers' control had been trampled on, smashed to smithereens by a Stalinist counter-revolution in the late 1920s. And what had emerged was a bureaucratic state with all the fundamental features of capitalism: a tiny minority ruling and exploiting the vast majority in order not to provide for people, but to accumulate more and more wealth in the hands of the ruling minority. Cliff called it state capitalism. The driving force was competition, in this instance, military competition with the West. Now the arguments and theory Trotsky had established in his stand against Stalin could be developed to a new level. This is the theoretical foundation of this brief account of the revolution.

While not replying explicitly to every historian of the revolution, this account will answer alternative interpretations, because the most popular and widely propagated arguments – in academia, in schools, in popular culture and even in most left-wing accounts – serve not historical truth, but a political agenda. As one writer concluded: "[N]o other subject of historical research and debate has been more directly conditioned by conscious political manipulation".[5]

The most common agenda is to discredit the very idea that workers could run the world and make a better fist of it than the capitalist jackals who are destroying people's lives and life itself on this planet. It is to convince us that socialism isn't possible, or that if you build a party that can lead workers to power, it will only end in dictatorship. However, even most left-wing historians until the radicalisation of the 1960s, influenced by the deadening influence of Stalinism, could not grasp the essential truths of the events of 1917. They tended to draw a picture of the heroic Lenin leading an authoritarian Bolshevik Party fulfilling the pre-ordained destiny of the Russian masses. Both these versions agreed that Stalin was the inheritor of Lenin's mantle. The only disagreement was whether this was an admirable or a horrific outcome.

And both led away from mobilising to fight for workers' power. Who would want to struggle only to repeat Stalin's totalitarian state if their desire is for human freedom? This association discredited Marxism for generations. It's not hard to see that the beneficiaries of these ideas are those who have a stake in this barbarous society, the capitalist ruling class, both in the West and in the so-called "Communist" countries.

The strength of Cliff's position is that it puts workers' revolution back at the centre of the struggle for socialism. It repudiates all the arguments which locate the origins of Stalin's dictatorship in the Bolshevik Party of Lenin. Most historians have looked at the revolution of 1917 through the distorting prism of Stalinism, whether from a sympathetic or hostile point of view. Cliff's view of Stalin's rule enables us to recognise the events of 1917 as a workers' revolution from below and to draw the lessons it can teach us for future struggles.

With the fracturing of the Stalinist monolith – beginning with the Hungarian Revolution in 1956 and gathering pace during the radicalisation of the 1960s as it became clear that the "Communism" of the East was as much a fraud as the "freedom" of the West – new approaches were possible. Social historians began looking at the revolution "from below". They debunked much of the earlier histories, bringing the activity of masses of workers, peasants and soldiers into relief.[6] However because the genuine traditions of revolutionary Marxism were marginalised, few of them fully understood the class struggle and the relationship between the development of objective social forces and the subjective factors such as intentions and organisation of the oppressed. So many of them still could not explain the role of the Bolsheviks, the one revolutionary organisation which won mass support and was capable of leading the October insurrection which established workers' power. And so they were ill-equipped to defend their insights in response to the right-wing backlash against the radical hopes of the sixties.

Since the last decade of the twentieth century, overtly right-wing histories of the 1917 revolution have become the dominant influence on both academic and popular interpretations.[7] Richard Pipes' work, which drew a caricature of the "dark masses" of Russia manipulated by the authoritarian Bolsheviks, was enthusiastically promoted by the media as a masterpiece in spite of attempts to show that it ignored a whole body of recent rigorous investigation. It was as if "a veil was to be drawn over the implications of the best work of recent decades in an attempt to ensure that popular understanding of the revolution, in the East and West alike, would be based on old myths resuscitated".[8] Orlando Figes was more than happy to oblige. In his *People's Tragedy, the Russian Revolution 1891–1924*, an epic tome and widely publicised as the last word on the revolution, he dismisses the October Revolution as "in reality such a small-scale event, being in effect no more than a military coup, that it passed unnoticed by the vast majority of inhabitants of Petrograd". What better way to draw a veil over the event which inspired millions to try to change the world for the better.[9]

War is a relentless background to life in twenty-first century capitalism, the "war on terror" promotes racism and denial of human rights, poverty *increases* in the wealthiest countries such as the US and Australia in the midst of supposed booms, to say nothing of the misery in the poorest places, the destruction of the environment – need we go on? So the desire for a decent life will again and again lead to challenges to the rule of capital. The question is not *whether* it will happen – just read the history of capitalism so far – but *when*. Then the problem will be whether the lessons from previous revolutionary challenges to capitalism have been brought together in a way that ensures the vast mass of humanity take things into their own hands, making socialism possible.

The stakes are high: socialism or barbarism, in the prophetic words of the Polish-German revolutionary, Rosa Luxemburg. It is essential that anyone who wants to take the challenge up to the capitalists is armed with the arguments to defeat the most dominant interpretations of the events of Russia in 1917 and the ideas we will need to win the fight. That is the reason to study the Russian Revolution.

The aim of this small book is to provide a narrative accessible to those who are not familiar with the events, but in a way that offers a revolutionary Marxist interpretation. So I hope that those who are familiar with the narrative, and with the debates about it, will also find it useful and convincing.

Introduction

If future historians look for the group that began the Russian Revolution, let them not create any involved theory. The Russian Revolution was begun by hungry women and children demanding bread and herrings. They started by wrecking tram cars and looting a few small shops. Only later did they, together with workmen and politicians, become ambitious to wreck that mighty edifice the Russian autocracy.[10]

By providing, almost by accident, a large-scale instance of unpunished civil disorder, they [the working-class women of Petrograd] demonstrated the hopeless inability of the government to preserve law and order at the centre of its power.[11]

THERE EXISTED THE CONDITIONS that Lenin, leader of the Bolsheviks, thought were necessary for a revolutionary situation: the masses would not go on in the old ways and the ruling classes could not continue to rule in the old ways. We owe a great tribute to the women workers of Petrograd on International Working Women's Day 1917. And that is where our narrative begins.

It will then follow the main events of 1917 and discuss the marvellous achievements of masses of workers as they tried to take their destiny into their own hands: the creation of the soviets or workers' councils, the most democratic organisations yet seen by humanity since the division of society into classes about 6,000 years ago. We will see that the February Revolution did not establish workers' rule, but a provisional government which represented the interests of the capitalists. In the standoff between the soviets and the government the war dragged on, the peasants craved in vain for the land and workers' conditions continued to worsen.

When Lenin returns to Russia from exile in April, he will have to rely on the class instincts of the worker members of his Bolshevik Party in order to combat the conservatism of the leading members and reorient the party to see that the government will have to be overthrown in order to get land, bread and peace. We will experience the impatience of the most militant workers and soldiers in Petrograd in July and Lenin's attempts to restrain them for fear of a premature challenge to the new provisional government.

The narrative will highlight the inhumanity of those who rule, their cruelty, their absolute ruthlessness when faced with the possibility that they will not rule. It will follow the Bolsheviks into hiding and jail, see their printing presses smashed. The liberal press will smear their name with lies. We will see how the capitalists deliberately sabotaged industry to discredit the revolution, and that they backed an attempted military coup by General Kornilov in August. On the other side we will see the revolutionary actions of the workers that defeated Kornilov's coup in four days. Then we will examine the great victory of October 1917 over those who backed capitalist rule.

Finally we will have to face the tragedy that befell the revolution. It was not the result of some timeless human failing, nor was it the consequence of a coup by a small minority as most historians would have us believe. The failure of the revolutionary movements across Europe explains this catastrophe. We will answer the main arguments that aim to discredit the revolution by denigrating the Bolshevik Party which led the October insurrection.

Spontaneous revolution?

The diarist we began with, like many writers, thought that women rising up for bread and herrings makes a mockery of the efforts of revolutionaries to prepare for revolution, and that it contradicts Marxism. On the contrary, it confirms some of the central Marxist tenets. Marx, and all those revolutionaries who have followed in his footsteps, understood that revolutions don't simply happen because of revolutionaries' arguments. It is the lived experience of oppression, exploitation, poverty, misery and yet a determination to survive that pushes people into revolutionary situations. All of the great workers' revolutions since the Paris Commune of 1871 have erupted as working people have tried to minimise the effects of capitalist crisis on their lives.[12]

To recognise the spontaneity involved in revolution does not in any way detract from the importance of the role of conscious leaders, organisations and the levels of determination among the mass of workers. All of these come into play, precisely because revolutions develop as a result of economic, political and social conditions, drawing in hundreds of thousands of the oppressed who have not spent the previous years of their life pondering over how to defeat their oppressors. Revolutions happen because of "spontaneous" uprisings, but it is the level of conscious organisation by a minority beforehand that determines whether workers can defeat their class enemies and consolidate their rule. The actions of the women workers in Petrograd in February 1917 are of great historical importance, but they are not unique in the history of workers' uprisings.

What was unique was the existence of a political organisation, the Bolsheviks, painstakingly built for years by revolutionaries who, by participating in the victories, defeats, repression and suffering of the masses, had brought together the most advanced and class-conscious workers. Their organisation played the decisive role in the final victory in October. But they had virtually no Bolshevik women's organisation in February – or any organisation to speak of – because many of the leading Bolsheviks had been in jail since 1915 or in exile. They were in fact freed by the women's February uprising.

Nevertheless, in spite of being taken by surprise in February, the Bolsheviks, who had learnt to appraise any political situation and act on that, rather than pipe dreams and false hopes, played a vital role. They led the masses of workers and soldiers in the cities through the various crises and turning points of 1917 to an understanding that the provisional government had to be overthrown in order to end the war, give the land to the peasants and fulfil the demands of workers for an eight-hour day, dignity and a decent life.

It is the Bolsheviks' role that helps explain the difference between the February and the October Revolutions. October was the end result of a process of developing mass class consciousness. In February, hundreds of thousands came into the streets with little idea of what might come of their actions and with the simple demands of bread for their families and an end to the world war. The October Revolution was highly organised and premeditated. Its slogan reflected the program of the Bolsheviks for achieving those simple demands: "All power to the soviets of workers, soldiers and peasants deputies!" The lack of street mobilisations leads most historians to declare October a Bolshevik coup. On the contrary, this lack of public display reflects not less mass involvement, but an increased understanding and support for the revolution which meant the provisional government could find no support and the All Russian Congress of the Soviet of Workers', Soldiers' and Peasants' Deputies took power.

In spite of its overthrow by Stalin in the 1920s, the experience of the revolution of 1917 in Russia stands as a reminder of the possibility for a better world. The tragedy of its defeat does not invalidate the lessons the workers and peasants of Russia taught us by their heroic struggles. In fact, the defeat itself teaches us valuable lessons, not the least being that wherever we are, there is no more important task than to build an organisation capable of giving support to any revolution wherever it may erupt. That, in a nutshell, is the point of this book – to argue for this project, and to bring together in a brief publication the lessons any such organisation needs to incorporate into its political program if it is to pass the test when the time for revolution is upon it.

Chapter one
The February Revolution

O N 23 FEBRUARY 1917 (8 March by the Western calendar) in Petrograd, many thousands of angry working-class women celebrated International Working Women's Day (IWD hereafter) by holding meetings in their workplaces. Before the morning was out – in defiance of the leaders of all the left-wing political parties, including the revolutionary Bolsheviks who thought a mass strike premature and that it would only be crushed – tens of thousands were on strike.

Working women, joined by housewives, were marching through the streets and visiting workplaces where better-organised and experienced male workers might be expected to come out in sympathy with their demands for "bread!". A worker in the Nobel engineering plant in the Vyborg district, the centre of working-class radicalism and militancy, recalled a typical scene:

> We could hear women's voices in the lane overlooked by the windows ...: "Down with high prices!" "Down with hunger!" "Bread for the workers!" I and several comrades rushed at once to the windows ... The gates of No 1 Bol'shaia Sampsonievskaia mill were flung open. Masses of women workers in a militant frame of mind filled the lane. Those who caught sight of us began to wave their arms, shouting: "Come out!" "Stop work!" Snowballs flew through the windows. We decided to join the demonstration.[13]

The traditions of solidarity the women were banking on stood them in good stead. By the end of the day over 100,000, a third of the city's industrial workforce, were on strike in Petrograd.[14] A Bolshevik worker known only as Kayurov wrote later, "once there is a mass strike, one must call everybody into the streets and take the lead".

Leon Trotsky – the greatest historian of the revolution and one of its most popular and brilliant leaders – comments: Kayurov's testimony that "the idea of going into the streets had long been ripening among the workers; only at that moment nobody imagined where it would lead" is "important for understanding the mechanics of the events".[15]

The days which followed, in which working-class women continued to play a significant and leading role, were to result in the downfall of the repressive and hated tsar. They were the first steps taken towards the establishment of the first and only workers' state in history.

On the next day, 24 February, meetings, proclamations, marches continued as increasing numbers of workers joined the strike wave. By the end of the day 200,000 had swelled the ranks of the angry strikers demanding bread to feed their starving families. Most of the orators remain nameless, but thanks to the secret police some of the workers' contributions to these momentous events are preserved in archives of the very state which aimed to crush this insubordination and rebellion against "law and order". Peter Tikhonov is one such worker:

> So, comrades, we must quit our work today, support union with other comrades and go to get bread by ourselves. Comrades, my opinion is this. If we cannot get a loaf of bread for ourselves in a righteous way, then we must do everything: we must go ahead and solve our problems by force. Only in this way will we be able to get bread for ourselves. Comrades, remember this also. Down with the government! Down with the war![16]

So already, demands for bread arising from the starvation which is clearly linked to the war have moved on to more political demands. Or we might say, the demand for bread was not, as many historians think, "just" an "economic" demand, but a highly political one in the context of the horrors of the war and the sacrifices working families were making with their men away in the trenches.

On this day there was an important development. The soldiers seemed reluctant to fire on the demonstrating crowds. This was the question hanging over the movement. Would they be massacred as workers were in the 1905 revolution, or could they prevail? The elite

Cossacks seem to have been some of the first to waver. Workers from the Erikson factory, one of the main workplaces in the Vyborg district, 2,500 of them marching down a narrow street, were the first to test them: "Decisive moment!" says Trotsky. The horsemen rode through:

> "One of them smiled", Kayurov recalls, "and one of them gave the workers a good wink." This wink was not without meaning. The workers were emboldened with a friendly, not hostile kind of assurance, and slightly infected the Cossacks with it. The one who winked found imitators... The Cossacks, without openly breaking discipline, failed to force the crowd to disperse.

After repeated attempts by their officers to have the crowd attacked,

> standing stock still in perfect discipline, the Cossacks did not hinder the workers from "diving" under their horses. The revolution does not choose its paths; it made its first steps toward victory under the belly of a Cossack's horse. A remarkable incident! And remarkable the eye of its narrator – an eye which took an impression of every bend in the process. No wonder, for the narrator was a leader; he was at the head of over two thousand men.[17]

On the 25th, thousands of students joined the workers' demonstrations and now 240,000 were on strike. Trotsky pays due tribute to the women and their role in winning over the soldiers:

> A great role is played by women workers in the relation between workers and soldiers. They go up to the cordons more boldly than men, take hold of the rifles, beseech, almost command: "Put down your bayonets – join us." The soldiers are excited, ashamed, exchange anxious glances, waver; someone makes up his mind first, and the bayonets rise guiltily above the shoulders of the advancing crowd. The barrier is opened, a joyous and grateful "Hurrah!" shakes the air. The soldiers are surrounded. Everywhere arguments, reproaches, appeals – the revolution makes another forward step.[18]

Ariadna Tyrkova was a liberal journalist and Cadet (Constitutional Democrats, party of the liberal bourgeoisie) politician, wife of a wealthy English businessman. She recorded her upper-class distaste of "the mob in the labour districts...looting the markets and parading the streets with shouts of 'bread!'". On the other hand she was affected by the sense of joy and hope for a new world that erupted: "in those days good-nature and good-will were general, and created a strong, common feeling, breathing energy and force. People looked joyfully and trustfully into each other's eyes and smiled with that irrepressible happy smile which beams on lovers' faces". On perhaps the third day of the revolution, a telegraph messenger, "pale, tired out, sickly, hollow-cheeked" handed her a telegram and surprised her with "Thank you so much". In answer to her "what for?" he summed up how thousands must have been feeling:

> "We know about it", he said warmly, "although we are small people, and have kept to our slums afraid to move, still we knew of what others did. I have read your articles in the paper and heard your speeches at meetings ... Thank God, we've gained our liberty, you and I. It seems to me as if I were born again ... I seem to tread on air, my very soul seems to sing – I am a man, I am no longer a slave but a free man."[19]

On the 26th, unlike some troops who were on the point of mutiny, the Volynsky Guard fired on a crowd; but only to retreat to their barracks feeling guilty about the horrendous step they had taken. They spent most of the night debating what to do. When their officers arrived at 8am the troops had decided they would not take orders to shoot at the protesters again. They shot their commanding officer and set out for other barracks to agitate for a general mutiny. By the afternoon of the 27th hundreds of thousands of workers, soldiers, students, and housewives were in the streets. And many of them were armed. The government authority collapsed. A revolution begun by working women, some of the most oppressed and downtrodden in Russian society, had deposed one of the most authoritarian regimes in Europe.

Why was there was a revolution?

How did this happen? Students who study the Russian Revolution are usually invited to discuss the question: was the February Revolution "spontaneous", or was it "organised"? And if the latter, who led it? Many millions of words have been printed discussing this riddle. The question is based on the assumption that "spontaneity" and "organisation" are counterposed. But this does not help clarify the issue, it only confuses it. The February Revolution was, like all others, both spontaneous and organised, with leaders who contributed to its success (or failure in other cases).

Before most revolutions, very few people expect the coming upheavals. Even Lenin, who devoted his life to preparing for a revolution, had declared just a few months earlier that he did not expect it to happen in his lifetime. The mundane routine of life can hide the growing discontent below the surface until some event or issue acts as a spark to increasingly volatile tinder. So in Russia, from 1912 there had been a growing strike wave which signalled a revival of working-class militancy after the terrible years of repression which followed the crushing of the 1905 revolution. But the outbreak of World War I struck a blow against the rising struggles. Because the Bolsheviks were intransigently opposed to the war, in Russia unlike in most other countries, there was working-class resistance. But middle-class hysterical patriotism made it difficult to build a broad movement. The Bolsheviks' isolation was made all the harder to bear because of the betrayal by all of the main socialist parties around Europe (grouped in the Second International), except in Italy and a few small parties such as the Serbian and the Independent Labour Party in Britain. Party after party which had given lip service to the rhetoric against imperialist war and threats to turn any such war into a war on their own ruling classes, called for their members and supporters to go off and kill workers of the other belligerent countries.

But the war brought poverty and misery to millions of workers and peasants as they eked out a living on what women could earn. In the trenches the men suffered terribly. Of course, as in all wars, the rich in the cities and landlords in the country were not starving. War profits for 1914 and 1915 showed who benefited from the misery of the masses: the Moscow textile company of the Riabushinskys showed a net profit of 75 percent; the Tver Company, 111 percent; the copper works of Kolchugin netted over 12 million on a basic capital of 10 million. Who better than Trotsky to describe the obscenity of it:

> Speculation of all kinds and gambling on the market went to the point of paroxysm. Enormous fortunes arose out of the bloody foam. The lack of bread and fuel in the capital did not prevent the court jeweller Faberget from boasting that he had never before done such a flourishing business. Lady-in-waiting Vyrubova says that in no other season were such gowns to be seen as in the winter of 1915–16, and never were so many diamonds purchased. The night clubs were brim full of heroes of the rear, legal deserters, and simply respectable people too old for the front but sufficiently young for the joy of life. ... A continual shower of gold fell from above. "Society" held out its hands and pockets, aristocratic ladies spread their skirts high, everybody splashed about in the bloody mud – bankers, heads of the commissariat, industrialists, ballerinas of the tsar and the grand dukes, orthodox prelates, ladies-in-waiting, liberal deputies, generals of the front and rear, radical lawyers, illustrious mandarins of both sexes, innumerable nephews, and more particularly nieces. All came running to grab and gobble, in fear lest the blessed rain should stop. And all rejected with indignation the shameful idea of a premature peace.[20]

Bread shortages in Petrograd were simply the issue that lit the fuse of simmering discontent. In all revolutions, the original "spontaneous" rebellion can always be explained by growing discontent if only we look beneath the appearance of calm. When workers and other oppressed groups take action they give voice to what is hidden from a superficial glance. However, there is often evidence of preparation and political activity among at least some layers of the population which give the spontaneity a degree of organisation.

The IWD demonstrations took place not just in the context of suffering, but also of an atmosphere of tension and class conflict. The year had begun with a mass strike on 9 January, the anniversary of the massacre of Petrograd workers on Bloody Sunday 1905, by around 140,000 workers from at least 120 factories – 40 percent of the Petrograd industrial workers. On 14 February another major strike of 84,000 closed down more than 52 factories in the midst of fears by the middle class that there would be "clashes" at the reopening of the Duma (parliament). One historian says "strikes and demonstrations became daily events, with student demonstrations at Petrograd's higher educational institutions and strikes in other cities adding to the growing turmoil". And on 22 February, the day before IWD, 30,000 workers had been locked out by management at the giant Putilov works, Russia's largest plant. A protest demonstration was prevented by police; and workers who met with Alexander Kerensky, a liberal in the Duma (and who will play a crucial role later) warned him that this might be the beginning of a big political movement and that "something very serious might happen".[21]

At least some women were preparing for months before, weighing up the odds, assessing their actions and options. Since 1915 there had been "bread riots" or "food pogroms" by working-class women. On 6 April 1915 women smashed and looted a Petrograd meat market when the sale of meat was suspended for a day. Two days later women in Moscow were just as militant over bread shortages. In June 1915, a strike in Ivanovo-Vosnesensk began as a "flour strike"; a month later it had developed into a political movement to end the war and free jailed workers. Thirty people were killed. In Kostromo at the same time, a strike was fired at. This in turn led to a funeral and another strike. This time the women sent a circular to the soldiers asking them for protection instead of bullets.[22]

By January 1917 food queues were intolerable, working women were expected to keep their families together and alive with their husbands, brothers, fathers and sons at the front from where the news was horrific. A police report to their superiors in January 1917 bears witness to workers' suffering. It stated that Russia's working class was "on the edge of despair..."

> [T]he slightest explosion, however trivial its pretext, will lead to uncontrollable riots... The inability to buy goods, the frustrations of queuing, the rising death rate owing to poor living conditions, and the cold

and damp produced by lack of coal...have all created a situation where most of the workers are ready to embark on the savage excesses of a food riot.[23]

Preparing for revolution

Many historians only notice that the women's uprising seems spontaneous and in defiance of the socialist organisations, and so they obscure the level of agitation and preparation for a "manifestation". The strike in the huge Putilov works had lit a fuse. To some extent the very fact that the political organisations had refused to support mass protests on IWD indicates the level of tension. If there is no chance of a showdown with the authorities, why would they have not called everyone out with a view to trying to get some more food in the shops? What was their argument? Not that demonstrations are ineffective, or that they opposed a showdown, but that this would be *premature*, that they would be crushed. They simply wanted delay in order to keep organising.

We get glimpses of the preparations going on. A few days before IWD the largely female staff at the Vasilevsky Island trolley-car park sent a woman to the nearby 180th Infantry Regiment to ask the soldiers if they would fire on them if they came out. The answer was no, ensuring that on IWD the trolley-car workers joined the demonstration.

Again, the spies give us a window into the situation (and who better to observe the shifts in mood going on beneath the surface calm than those who spent their time spying on every sign of opposition):

> [M]others of families, exhausted from the endless queues at the shops, suffering at the sight of their sick and half-famished children, at this moment are much closer indeed to revolution than are Mssrs Milyukov, Rodichev, and Co. [liberal politicians]; and of course are more dangerous because they constitute a mass of inflammable matter for which only a spark is sufficient to cause it to burst into flames.[24]

The organising and preparation were not accidental, nor do they negate the importance of the element of spontaneity. They are part and parcel of the same picture. Workers were drawing conclusions from events. On the 23rd a police agent reported "the idea that an uprising is the only means to escape from the food crisis is becoming more and more popular among the masses".[25] Many of the political arguments, the initiative and foresight came from workers who had already experienced the revolution of 1905 and the aftermath when it was crushed. They knew that certain things had to be prepared, such as winning the soldiers over. In fact, this led to arguments among the activists. Many workers wanted to keep increasing the militancy in the streets. But Alexander Shliapnikov, the most prominent Bolshevik leader in Petrograd at the time, urged workers to instead put their efforts towards drawing the soldiers into the struggle, a more political task which required more patience, but a critical one.[26] Rex Wade, a social historian who has tried to understand the revolution by looking at the actions of the workers, says:

> Especially important were the factory activists... Drawing on lengthy strike experience they quickly moved to the fore and provided the organizational skills and leadership for the demonstrations of the next few days. They organized the columns of workers as they marched from the factories and exhorted workers to demonstrate rather than simply going home. They gave impassioned speeches articulating worker grievances and demanding the overthrow of the regime. These activists helped organize the strike committees and other revolutionary organizations.[27]

And many workers had been touched by the propaganda, agitation and political arguments of the Bolsheviks. Trotsky summed up the importance of the Bolsheviks in his *History of the Russian Revolution*, by implication admitting the momentous mistake he had made in standing aloof from Lenin's determination to build that organisation:

> The mystic doctrine of spontaneousness explains nothing. In order correctly to appraise the situation and determine the moment for a blow at the enemy, it was necessary that the masses or their guiding layers should make their examination of historical events and have their criteria for estimating them. In other words, it was necessary that there should be not masses in the abstract... It was necessary that throughout this

mass should be scattered workers who had thought over the experience of 1905, criticised the constitutional illusions of the liberals and Mensheviks [socialists to the right of the Bolsheviks], assimilated the perspectives of the revolution, meditated hundreds of times about the question of the army, watched attentively what was going on in its midst – workers capable of making revolutionary inferences from what they observed and communicating them to others...

In every factory, each guild, in each company, in each tavern, in the military hospital... Everywhere were to be found the interpreters of events, chiefly from among the workers, from whom one inquired, "what's the news?" and from whom one awaited the needed words. These leaders had often been left to themselves, had nourished themselves upon fragments of revolutionary generalisations arriving in their hands by various routes, had studied out by themselves between the lines of the liberal papers what they needed... Elements of experience, criticism, initiative, self-sacrifice, seeped down through the mass and created, invisibly to a superficial glance but no less decisively, an inner mechanics of the revolutionary movement as a conscious process. To the smug politicians...everything that happens among masses is customarily represented as an instinctive process...

To the question, Who led the February Revolution? We can answer definitely enough: Conscious and tempered workers educated for the most part by the party of Lenin.[28]

Chapter two
The impact of the February Revolution

THE OVERTHROW OF THE HATED TSAR NICHOLAS II, "THE BLOODY", filled Petrograd's workers and soldiers with elation and expectations. Once they returned to the workplaces there was an outpouring of their hopes for a new society in the form of declarations drawn up by general meetings. One of the earliest conservative historians of the revolution had great insight into the process by which workers became radicalised. His account of the first months of the revolution gives a feel for the level of self-activity:

> What were the outstanding characteristics of the first period of the "deepening of the revolution"? Loosening of discipline in the army, increasingly radical demands of the industrial workers, first for higher wages, then for control over production and distribution, arbitrary confiscations of houses in the towns, and, to a greater degree, of land in the country districts, insistence in such non-Russian parts of the country as Finland and Ukrainia on the grant of far reaching autonomy.[29]

Everything seemed turned on its head and anything was possible. The expectations were not just for political democracy while the social power of the capitalists remained. This is reflected in the fact that it was not the national flag, but the red flag of socialism that fluttered everywhere, including on official buildings. Significantly, the international socialist holiday, May Day, was institutionalised as an official holiday. The workers of the Dinamo works summed up aspirations widely held:

> The people and the army went onto the streets not to replace one government by another, but to carry out our slogans. These slogans are

"Freedom", "Equality", "Land and Liberty" and "An End to the Bloody War".
For us, the unpropertied classes, the bloody slaughter is unnecessary.[30]

The records don't show whether this was a cautionary note, whether they foresaw that the struggle was only beginning. Nevertheless, it clearly laid out their goals and expectations. But workers did not limit themselves to proclamations. They began the task of creating new organs of power at every level of society: factory committees, trade unions, and the beginnings of workers' armed militias to keep order. They immediately began setting up workers' councils, or soviets, drawing on the experience of the 1905 revolution.

And Petrograd was not alone. News of the rebellion sparked strikes in Moscow late on 27 February. Where Petrograd had experienced several days of street demonstrations and strikes, almost overnight Moscow caught up. Within 48 hours police stations had been wrecked by crowds of workers and students, political prisoners freed and a Moscow soviet created. In response the government declared that the rioting by rabble must be put down. The soldier Shishilin says "but by this time, the soldiers understood the word rabble in the opposite sense".[31] By 2pm on the 28th many soldiers had arrived at the building of the city Duma enquiring how to join the revolution.

In fact, it was the news that Moscow had joined the uprising that pushed the tsar to concede defeat. It was obvious his regime had no mass support in either of the centres of industrial, economic, political and social power, and no armed force with which to impose its will.

The revolution brought the reality of class rule and the exploitation it rested on out from the recesses of respectable society. Decades of oppression and the hatred it breeds drove workers to take their chance at a better life. They challenged capitalist rule by demanding the eight-hour day, decent wages, equal wages for women workers with men. They campaigned for better safety, for meal breaks, sick leave, and reform of hiring practices. They often burned factory rule books and lists of fines and other punishments for breaking the humiliating rules of the old order.[32] They demanded they be treated with respect. And to make their point, workers, especially women, spent the first weeks after the revolution throwing out managers known for humiliating workers. Those who got the worst treatment had a reputation for sexual harassment of female workers. Women would dump them in wheelbarrows, cart them out of their factory and if a river was nearby, dump them in it. Other acts of spontaneous joy which amounted to defiance infuriated the rich and respectable. They complained that servants were completely unruly, spending their time going out decked in red ribbons, coming home at all hours, going out again, and ignoring their employers' need to be waited on hand and foot.

In workplaces around Russia workers formed factory committees which organised everything from the soap in the washrooms, to fixing light bulbs, organising rosters, outlawing excessive overtime, disciplining unruly workers, controlling drunkenness, the presentation of cultural events and organising political discussions; and of course, taking control of production. The eight-hour day was not just an "economic" demand. It was regarded as central to enable workers to participate in the necessary social, political and cultural development which workers craved and to which they felt entitled.[33]

As an indication of the advances which accompany such social upheaval we only need to look at some of the innovations these committees arranged. "Democracy" did not just mean a new government, or elections, it meant control from below and participation in all areas of society, including the theatre and the schools. Even the church was affected. Some of the hierarchy who were not overwhelmed with horror turned to a version of Christian socialism. One of the more radical clergy, Vvendenskii, was elected to the Petrograd Soviet. He argued "the struggle on behalf of the poor is a basic principle of socialism, and it is our own Christian struggle". The Orthodox Church even created a "Committee on Bolshevism in the Church".[34] Morgan Philips Price, an English journalist in Russia at the time, recorded how in Samara

> the revolution had penetrated into the sacred precincts of the monastery; the monks had gone on strike and had turned out the abbot, who had gone off whining to the Holy Synod... On enquiry into the ideas entertained

by the monks for developing their little revolution, I found that they had already entered into an arrangement with the local peasantry. They were to keep enough land for themselves to work, and the rest was to go into the local commune. Thus a new monastic commune was in process of formation.[35]

You wonder how many provincial cities, monasteries, villages, workplaces, schools and universities were transformed by similar sentiments and arrangements. The examples we know of are only those that were recorded by accidents of fate; a foreign journalist who happened to be in the right place at the right time, a police record that survived, a scrap of a government report. It is like looking through a keyhole, a tantalising glimpse that makes us want to know what is in the rest of the room.

The self-activity of urban workers is somewhat better recorded. Women in particular played a prominent role in ensuring workers didn't work excessive hours, insisting that other workers should have the right to jobs and everyone should have time to participate in the revolutionary activities. When they couldn't force employers to pay equal wages, some committees collected a levy from the best paid which was then redistributed to the lowest paid, often women. This was their way of demonstrating that they were intent on building a new society in which human dignity was paramount.[36] Students were brought in to teach workers to read and write. One young woman taught workers to read by printing huge Bolshevik slogans on the blackboard each day.[37]

John Reed, the famous American writer, would immortalise these strivings for culture, knowledge and control over their lives in his *Ten Days that Shook the World*. He told the world "all Russia was learning to read, and *reading*":

> [T]he first six months, went out every day tons, car-loads, train-loads of literature, saturating the land. Russia absorbed reading matter like hot sand drinks water, insatiable. And it was not fables, falsified history, diluted religion, and the cheap fiction that corrupts – but social and economic theories, philosophy, the works of Tolstoy, Gogol, and Gorky.

He tells the story of arriving in Riga...

> where gaunt and bootless men sickened in the mud of desperate trenches; and when they saw us they started up. With their pinched faces and the flesh showing blue through their torn clothing, demanding eagerly, "did you bring anything to *read*?"

But it wasn't just reading, it was also "the Talk, beside which Carlyle's 'flood of French speech' was a mere trickle". Lectures, meetings, debates, in the factories, the barracks, in theatres or any other venue available: "what a marvellous sight to see the Putilov Factory pour out its forty thousand to listen to ... anybody, whatever they had to say, as long as they would talk!" Every street corner was a tribune, tram carriages, railway stations, wherever people gathered, could become the scene of impromptu debates.[38] When you imagine this ferment, this involvement, it is not difficult to visualise Lenin the night in October when he could stand his isolation in hiding no longer. In defiance of the Bolshevik Central Committee, he left his hiding place and headed into the city. His bodyguard, terrified at the time, left an account of Lenin quizzing a tram conductress about the state of affairs in the city. When he discovered she was left-wing, he began discussing strategy for the transfer of power to the soviets with her!

The upheavals in working life, along with expectations for a new way of living, impacted on personal relationships. A story from July gives us a glimpse. Women in a food queue were indifferent to the appeals of feminist, bourgeois women agitating for universal suffrage for the election of the Constituent Assembly. It's easy to see why – women workers voted and participated in the factory councils and soviet elections, and these were their institutions. But when a soldier smirked "Does that mean I can't hit my wife?" – "[A]t this the crowd livened up. 'Oh, no, you don't honey'. They shouted. 'None of that. You just try it. Nothing doing. Let ourselves be beaten any more? Not on your life. Nobody has the right now'".[39]

It was not only workers who were asserting their rights, experimenting with new ways of living and giving their supposed "superiors" a taste of democracy. John Reed recorded how the soldiers, through elected committees, learnt to stand up to their officers. When the government tried to enforce discipline in the army after the February days, the Petrograd Soviet of Workers' Deputies was forced by the sheer rage of the soldiers to pass what famously became known as "Order No.1" in its first session. It promoted a complete restructuring of the army and the relationships between soldiers and their officers. Disrespectful or demeaning address by the officers was forbidden, the soldiers' committees recognised and the death penalty abolished.

Word spread like wildfire about the momentous events in Petrograd. Morgan Philips Price wrote to his wife on 13 March from Tiflis, in the Caucasus: "Most exciting times. I knew this was coming sooner or later but did not think it would come so quickly. Have been running about the Caucasus for last fortnight attending revolutionary meetings... Whole country is wild with joy".[40]

A week later he wrote to the *Manchester Guardian* that news of the dissolution of the Duma, the old tsarist parliament "was the signal for revolt..."

> The railwaymen of Tiflis and the oil workers of Baku prepared for a general strike... [I]ntense suppressed excitement all over the Caucasus... [P]reparations were made for a great mass meeting at Tiflis on Sunday, 18 March. That morning telegrams had been received ordering the abolition of the secret police, the release of all political prisoners, and the handing over of all civil affairs to the municipalities and rural councils.

His description of the mass meeting was typical of the exhilarating reports that raced around the globe inspiring workers with the hope that this was the beginning of a new world. It is a living memory of how the most far-flung, even backward corners of the tsarist empire were brought to their feet, thrilled by the promise of a new society in which the oppressed would now determine their own future:

> Here had assembled almost every element in the multi-racial population of this part of the Empire. There were wild mountain tribes, Lesgians, Avars, Chechens, and Swanetians in their long black cloaks and sheepskin caps. In the recesses of the Caucus range, where their homes lie, the eddies of

the waves of revolution had swept. Sunk in patriarchal feudalism until recently, many of them did not know whether they were subjects of the Tsar of Russia or of the Sultan of Turkey. Yet they had come walking across miles of mountain tracks to pay their humble tribute to the great Russian Revolution.

Georgian peasants, many of them influenced by modern Western thought including Marxism, came in their wagons. They were joined by liberal Armenian merchants, Tartar peasants from the East Caucasus with their memories of the Persian revolutionary movement of 1908-09, and industrial workers with their potential social and economic power over the railways and oilfields. Side by side they stood with poets, students, doctors and the like.

> Here in the great concourse of Caucasian peoples were standing side by side the most primitive and the most progressive types of the human race. For years they have been sunk in apathy, fatalism and scepticism and their racial feuds have been purposely fomented by the old Government. Now the flood of their combined intellect and energy had burst forth and broken the rotten banks of privilege and oppression ... a great concourse of medieval mountaineers and twentieth century proletariat, all inspired by one idea – brotherhood and freedom.[41]

Chapter three
February: the unfinished revolution

> Whole country is wild with joy, waving red flags and singing Marseillaise (the French revolutionary anthem). It has surpassed my wildest dreams, and I can hardly believe it's true...
>
> Long live Great Russia, who has shown the world the road to freedom. May Germany and England follow in her steps.[42]

So wrote Morgan Philips Price of the spirit of the heady days in February. However, the victory of the workers did not ensure the end of class society. The struggle, magnificent as it was, had only just begun. Trotsky concluded his comments about the role of the Bolsheviks quoted at the end of chapter one with this: "But we must here immediately add: their leadership proved sufficient to guarantee the victory of the insurrection, but it was not adequate to transfer immediately into the hands of the proletarian vanguard the leadership of the revolution".

The situation which resulted from the February Revolution is known, not just by Marxists, as "dual power". It is not unique to Russia in 1917, but has existed in many revolutions where workers have challenged the ruling class for power, but not actually destroyed all the vestiges of the institutions used by the old ruling class to maintain their authority in society.[43]

In Russia, the dual power existed between the soviets (the councils set up by workers), and the provisional government, made up of former members of the old tsarist Duma. This provisional government was essentially the government of the bourgeoisie or capitalist class. The liberal-minded capitalists wanted reforms such as the establishment of a republic and parliamentary democracy. But the whole class was closely tied to the huge, aristocratic landowning class who backed the old tsarist regime; and they were beholden to foreign capitalists for financial loans. They wanted to be in power and more fully develop capitalism. But their dilemma was that their ties made them terrified of the very revolution which could bring down the tsar. How could capitalists support a revolution that raised workers and peasants to their feet when their reactionary allies and backers were breathing down their necks demanding they safeguard their profits and power?

The workers had made the revolution in spite of them. This meant the situation was very confused. Capitalists and their supporters in the middle classes, and even some big land owners, used the phrases of the revolution to avoid total isolation. Many of their aspirations were fulfilled by the February Revolution – greater freedoms, civil rights, the prospect of a democratic parliamentary regime. However they were intent on limiting the social results of that revolution. For one thing they tended to be patriotic, and so hoped now they could strengthen the war effort and defeat Germany. On the home front they wanted nothing more than the right to exploit their workers, to manage the capitalist economy in their own interests, and to modernise the political structures of Russia accordingly. Workers had little place in this scheme of things other than to work to produce their profits.

On 1 March the new government elected a ministry of which Trotsky says: "The fact is, with one single exception, the revolution accomplished by workers and soldiers found no reflection whatever in the staff of the revolutionary government". The exception was Kerensky, who as Trotsky says "was not a revolutionist", but more of "a provincial lawyer who had defended political cases". Prince Lvov – a *prince!* – was appointed prime minister. He was reported, on arriving at Vyborg, a centre of working-class militancy, to have fallen sick. His sickness was "attributed to the emotional condition in which he found himself". Trotsky comments sarcastically; "the prince was evidently not built for revolutionary excitement". Trotsky sums up the results of the machinations of the upper classes as they tried to get control into their own hands:

> Thus as a result of a victorious insurrection of workers and soldiers, there

appeared at the helm of government a handful of the very richest landlords and industrialists, remarkable for less than nothing, political dilettantes without a programme – and at the head of them a prince with a strong dislike for excitement.[44]

However, "among the workers and soldiers the composition of the government created an immediate feeling of hostility, or at the best a dumb bewilderment". So, masses of workers, soldiers, the poor and oppressed rallied to the soviets. Trotsky recalls: "In the eyes of those masses the Soviet was an organised expression of their distrust of all who had oppressed them".[45]

These factory committees, and the district and central soviets to which they elected delegates, posed a threat to the ability of the ruling class to rule. Social historian Rex Wade says:

> [M]any worker resolutions expressed distrust of any government composed of members of the upper class... This attitude reflected not only social hostility and the influence of the socialist parties, but that in the eyes of many workers real legitimacy and authority rested with the soviets, Petrograd and local. They often ignored the government altogether, with factory resolutions more likely to call on the Soviet than the government to deal with issues. From there it was only a short step to resolutions calling for a government based on the soviets, for "Soviet Power".[46]

Even in the first days of the new government, motions that revealed a healthy scepticism about the government of the class enemy were regularly passed by workers' meetings. This one from the Izhora works was typical:

> All measures of the provisional government that destroy the remnants of the autocracy and strengthen the freedom of the people must be fully supported by the democracy. All measures that lead to conciliation with the old regime and that are directed against the people must meet with decisive protest and counteraction.[47]

One of the key issues which drove the uprising of February was the passionate desire for peace that gripped the masses. They also anticipated that the land would be distributed to the peasants and workers would control industry. On the other hand, the provisional government was determined to continue to fight the imperialist war which had created the revolutionary crisis, determined to maintain their private property, and to consolidate their rule. They were merely biding their time. However, their own records highlight their precarious position, and the strength of the soviets. Guchkov, the minister of war, admitted to his chief of staff General Alexeiev, "[t]he government has no real power: the troops, the railroads, the post and telegraph are in the hands of the Soviet. The simple fact is that the provisional government exists only so long as the Soviet permits it".[48] Sukhanov, a moderate socialist who eventually joined the left Mensheviks, gives a picture of the situation in his memoirs:

> [A] victorious and profoundly democratic revolution...had made the proletariat the actual masters of the situation, while at the same time leaving untouched both the foundations of the bourgeois order and even the formal authority of the old ruling classes... [H]ow difficult, crucial, and ticklish the labour problem was at this period, and what experience, firmness, tact, and skill it required, between the hammer and the anvil, between the protesting rebellious workers and the employers, endlessly threatening strikes and lockouts.[49]

This situation could not last indefinitely – either those who live by exploiting the vast majority would claw back control or they would lose their power and the masses would begin the task of organising a new society. Exploiting classes cannot share power with those they exploit – why would the majority submit to a tiny minority (as the ruling class are) if they had access to power? This is not just an abstract analysis based on ideology. Both sides were to come to recognise this reality. In his history of 1917, Miliukov, the Cadet and leading figure of the provisional government, was to state "that the country was divided into two camps between which there could be no essential reconciliation or agreement".[50] The history of the months from February to October 1917 is about the struggle to resolve this standoff.

Workers' power

But before we look at the events which punctuate this struggle, it is important to look more closely at the embryo of workers' power. The soviets were then, and in every revolution where they have sprung out of workers' struggles, the most democratic institutions ever known. Delegates were elected in workplaces, in the barracks and in peasant villages. Today they would be elected in universities, schools and places like hospitals because of the huge numbers in these institutions. Delegates were recallable at any time, unlike the politicians we elect in parliamentary elections, who have fixed terms and can do whatever they please until close to the next election. Delegates remained in the workforce or army, and so shared the consequences of the decisions they voted for in the soviets. So they overthrew the separation of powers between legislative and administrative wings of government, so beloved of capitalist democracy, but so undemocratic and unaccountable. Delegates could not hide behind the actions of courts or bureaucrats. They had to take responsibility for their decisions. And workers exercised their democratic rights with enthusiasm. If delegates displeased their voters they were unceremoniously dumped.

For all these reasons, the political complexion of the soviets at any time gives a reasonable reflection of the level of class consciousness and what workers supported. For that reason, Lenin put paramount importance on who had a majority in the soviets. At the beginning of March, the first soviets were dominated by the moderate socialists and conservative representatives of the soldiers. Even the liberal bourgeoisie were pulled into the general euphoria of the mass movement. As Trotsky points out, the workers saw the soviets as the incarnation of the revolution, but "representatives of the possessing classes will also seek in the Soviet, with whatever grindings of teeth, protection and counsel in the resolving of conflicts".[51] The Bolsheviks commanded not more than a small minority in the soviets immediately after the February Revolution.

However it was not just the presence of outright exploiters in the government that confused the situation. The conservative or compromising socialists, such as the Mensheviks and Socialist Revolutionaries who dominated the Executive Committee of the Petrograd Soviet, added to the swirling array of ideas that made clarity of purpose virtually impossible. The scepticism towards the provisional government did not extend to the moderate socialists – the compromisers, as Trotsky calls them in his *History*. The dominance of the petty-bourgeois elements was what Trotsky calls the "paradox of February". On the one hand, the workers and soldiers had brought down the tsar, they looked to the soviets to represent their interests, and yet they trusted those who had no intention of realising the workers' aspirations. Trotsky likens "the petty-bourgeois democrats and socialists of the Sukhanov type, journalists and politicians of the new middle caste" to a "partition wall between the revolutionary masses and the capitalist bourgeoisie". They "had taught the masses that the bourgeoisie is an enemy, but themselves feared more than anything else to release the masses from the control of that enemy".[52]

In the coming months, it would take bitter experience for both the exploiters and their cohorts among the so-called socialists to be replaced by genuine representatives of the workers' interests. The representative numbers of the various parties always gave Lenin an assessment of whether the working class as a whole was ready to support a final revolution to resolve the standoff between the soviets and the provisional government. After all, the Bolsheviks were the only party clearly campaigning to transfer power to the soviets, to end the war and to give the land to the peasants. This stance was summed up in their slogan "land, bread and peace".

The reactionaries organise

At the end of the February Revolution, the bourgeoisie did not only have the provisional government as a centre of power. Immediately the liberal bourgeoisie began to think about how they could prevent the Soviet exercising unrestrained power. And the moderate socialists of the Socialist Revolutionaries and Mensheviks "took it for granted that the power ought to pass to the bourgeoisie".[53] The provisional government depended on the support of the moderate "socialist" leaders in the soviets. But its actual power base was the possessing classes who, as early as 10 March, constituted a Council of Trade and Industry, representing the united capitalists of Russia, to support the government. Even the Council of the United Nobility, who you might think had slunk off to oblivion after the overthrow of the monarchy, declared their united support for the provisional government, but significantly described it as "the sole lawful power in Russia". At the same time these parasitic classes began to muster all the influence, authority and resources they took for granted, and to denounce the "dual power". Every disturbance or disorder was blamed on this sharing of power.

The liberal press, supposedly for democratic rights and progress, opened a campaign "for a single sovereignty" – in other words, a campaign against the soviets and for the unchallenged rule of those who had been overthrown by the revolution.[54] The provisional government began to declare they would, at a suitable but unnamed date, call a "Constituent Assembly" which would embody this sole sovereignty. And, in the weasel words of official pronouncements, they made it clear that they intended to prosecute the hated imperialist war. Trotsky sums up: "So far as concerned the most threatening problems of the people's existence, the revolution had apparently been achieved only in order to make the announcement: everything remains as before".[55]

Procrastination met demands for the eight-hour day, and land for the peasants. But the problem for the provisional government was this: an insurrectionary mass could not easily be pacified without some redress of the misery and distress which had led to the revolution in the first place.

The problem on the workers' side was that it would take time and experience for increasing numbers and wider layers to see through the charlatans who had put themselves at the head of the soviets with honeyed phrases about "socialism". It would take time and experience for the masses to see that the only just solution to this situation of dual power was for them to take power into their own hands. But it would be some time before even the Bolsheviks raised the slogan "all power to the soviets", and even more before it had the deep-seated and broad support necessary to make that a reality.

Chapter four
The struggle for October

BEFORE 1917, TROTSKY WAS THE ONLY LEADING RUSSIAN MARXIST who thought the coming revolution would give workers the chance to take power and thereby begin the worldwide struggle for socialism. Lenin argued that because Russia was so backward, the revolution would be limited to establishing a democratic, capitalist republic. He agreed with Trotsky that the bourgeoisie would be incapable of leading their own revolution; they were too closely tied to the aristocracy through family and business interests, and they relied on the patently counter-revolutionary international bourgeoisie for loans and investment. And, crucially, they feared the power of the modern working class in the huge factories more than they hated the outdated monarchy.

However, once the February Revolution happened and the soviets were in a standoff with the provisional government, Lenin quickly dumped this limited perspective and argued that the working class had to prepare to take power. When he arrived back in Russia in early April he caused a storm among not just his enemies, but also the Bolshevik leadership themselves. The leaders who had been in Russia or arrived back before April, to the dismay of many of the worker members, supported the continuation of the war "to defend the revolution", and gave support to the provisional government. They had ignored Lenin's frantic letters which contradicted their arguments in *Pravda*, the Bolshevik paper, even refusing to publish some of them.

The Menshevik Sukhanov captures the flavour of the reaction to Lenin's return in his memoirs. The official "socialists" who had placed themselves at the head of the soviets and who were preaching moderation, turned out to welcome Lenin at the Finland train station. Cheidze, the Menshevik President of the Soviet, greeted him: "Comrade Lenin, in the name of the Petrograd Soviet and of the whole revolution we welcome you to Russia... But – we think that the principal task is the defence of the revolution..."

This "delicious but" as Sukhanov calls it, led to an appeal to Lenin for unity. Sukhanov continues:

> But Lenin knew exactly how to behave. He stood there as though nothing taking place had the slightest connexion with him ... turning away from [the soviet leaders] he made this "reply":

> "Dear Comrades, soldiers, sailors and workers! I...greet you as the vanguard of the worldwide proletarian army... The worldwide Socialist revolution has already dawned... The Russian revolution accomplished by you has prepared the way and opened a new epoch. Long live the worldwide Socialist revolution!"

Sukhanov sums up the experience: "Suddenly before the eyes of all of us, completely swallowed up by the routine drudgery of the revolution, there was presented a bright, blinding, exotic beacon obliterating everything we 'lived by'".[56]

Lenin declared, according to the outraged Sukhanov: "We don't need any parliamentary republic. We don't need any bourgeois democracy. We don't need any government except the Soviet of workers', soldiers' and farmhands' deputies!"

He attacked the Soviet majority, who were backing the provisional government as "the same old opportunists, speaking pretty words but in reality betraying the cause of socialism and the worker masses". Raskolnikov, a leading Bolshevik among the sailors, later wrote that Lenin's tactics laid down a Rubicon between the tactics of the leading Bolsheviks yesterday and the coming weeks.[57] Lenin spelled out his position in the *April Theses*, possibly the most important document of the revolution. He did not argue that the soviets could take power immediately. At the Petrograd Bolshevik conference of 14 April, he argued:

> The government must be overthrown, but not everybody understands this correctly. So long as the provisional government has the backing of the

Soviet of Workers' Deputies, you cannot "simply" overthrow it. The only way it can and must be overthrown is by winning over the majority of the Soviets.[58]

The Bolsheviks were clearly in a minority; only when the masses overwhelmingly supported the Bolsheviks' call for "all power to the soviets" would it be possible to take power and hold it. In the meantime, the task of the party was to "patiently explain".

Lenin reorients the Bolsheviks

Lenin was completely isolated among the leadership of the Bolsheviks. Contrary to the stereotype that has been created of the party – authoritarian, with Lenin acting as a petty dictator, his every decree carried out by unthinking followers – he had to fight for his position, and this he did with passionate determination. However, his efforts to turn the party around to a consistent revolutionary stance were all the easier because the worker members were in general agreement with him. They wanted an end to the war, the eight-hour day, and they supported the land being granted to the peasants. Moreover, they could see that the provisional government was not about to make any of these a reality. They protested vigorously against the right-wing positions taken by leaders such as Stalin, even demanding their expulsion from the party.

To convince the party to throw off the shackles of their wrong position, Lenin relied on their tradition of implacable hostility towards the ruling classes, and to the revolutionary instincts and understanding of the worker members. Lenin's absolute identification with the working class is the answer to the suspicious question raised by Sukhanov: "How did Lenin manage to outwit and conquer his Bolsheviks?" Sukhanov, the Menshevik, could not identify with the needs and aspirations of the workers and so he could not understand Lenin's quick victory. At the party conference of 24–29 April, a mere three weeks after Lenin's arrival, it was only a matter of endorsing Lenin's thesis that the soviets would have to take power. His position had already been endorsed by district after district.

Ludmilla Stahl, an Old Bolshevik, explained what it was like: "All the comrades before the arrival of Lenin were wandering in the dark", she said at the Petrograd conference of 14 April.

> We knew only the formulas of 1905. Seeing the independent creative work of the people, we could not teach them ... Our comrades could only limit themselves to ... parliamentary means, and took no account of the possibility of going further. In accepting the slogans of Lenin we are now doing what life itself suggests to us.[59]

The first glimpse of the counter-revolution

However, "life itself" presented difficulties immediately. Miliukov, the Cadet foreign minister in the provisional government, caused a storm when, on 18 April, traditionally celebrated as May Day (by the European calendar it was 1 May), he sent a note to the Allies which assured them that the peace-loving phrases they'd heard coming from his government should not give them any reason to think that the revolution which had taken place would lead to the weakening of Russia's role in the war. "Quite the contrary, the general aspiration of the whole people to bring the world war to a decisive victory has only been strengthened."[60]

This treachery did not become known straight away. On May Day all of Russia seemed united in celebrations, meetings and marches. Industry and state institutions were all closed for the festivities. Even tsarist generals who had remained at their posts marched under 1 May banners! News came from the trenches that soldiers on both sides sang revolutionary songs. In the cities prisoners of war took part in the processions, often singing the same songs in their own languages. As Trotsky describes it:

> [T]his immeasurable rejoicing, obliterating like a spring flood the delineation of classes, parties and ideas...was a vivid hope-giving fact which made it possible to believe that the revolution, in spite of all, did carry within itself the foundation of a better world.[61]

However, tension was in the background. On 17 April the soldiers began to realise that the Petrograd district staff were preparing to move the more revolutionary garrisons out of the city. The soldiers demanded these plans be put to rest. This was to become on ongoing question and source of conflict with authorities for the rest of the year, and would be posed more sharply with every new crisis.

For the masses the war was the root of all the evils they faced. The question hung in the air: when will the provisional government end the war? What are they waiting for? Trotsky again:

> [T]he masses are listening more and more attentively to the Bolsheviks, glancing at them obliquely, waitingly, some with half-hostility, others already with trust. Underneath the triumphal discipline of the demonstration the mood was tense. There was ferment in the masses.[62]

When Miliukov's note to the Allies became public, Petrograd was swept with outrage and indignation. On the 20th a mass demonstration dominated by banners with slogans such as "Down with the provisional government", "Down with Miliukov", "Down with the imperialist policy" marched to where the provisional government was sitting. "Exactly the same performance took place in Moscow too. Workers left their benches, soldiers their barracks. The streets and squares were seething with passion and tempestuous demonstrations", wrote Sukhanov.[63] The Bolsheviks were confronted with the difficult task of arguing that the only solution was for a transfer of power to the soviets, but that this was not possible until they had the backing of the countryside and wider layers of workers in other centres.

This was the beginning of the struggle for October. The deceit of the government was there for all to see. What did it mean? The Bolsheviks warned that the government did not want peace. Could they be right? On the other side, the counter-revolution began its open mobilisation. Taking confidence from the government's statement to the Allies and spurred into action by the workers' demonstration, the next day

> [t]he Nevsky, the chief artery of the bourgeoisie, was converted into a solid Cadet meeting. A considerable demonstration headed by the members

of the Cadet Central Committee marched to the Mariinsky Palace. Everywhere could be seen brand new placards, fresh from the sign printers: "Full Confidence to the Provisional Government!", "Long Live Miliukov!"... Under the flag of defence of the government, the first open and broad mobilisation of counter-revolutionary forces took place. In the centre of the town appeared trucks with armed officers, cadets and students.[64]

Continuing mass demonstrations of workers and soldiers in Petrograd clashed with this pro-war mobilisation. Shots were fired, either in confusion or in anger, perhaps both, and the first blood was shed since the February uprising. The facade of a united nation had been cracked open:

> Two worlds stood face to face. The patriotic columns called into the streets against the workers and soldiers by the Kadet Party consisted exclusively of the bourgeois layers of the population – officers, officials, intelligentsia. Two human floods – one for Constantinople, one for Peace – had issued from different parts of the town. Different in social composition, not a bit similar in external appearance, and with hostile inscriptions on their placards...[65]

During this melee, General Kornilov moved cannon into the Palace Square. This menacing move was thwarted by the provisional government, who could see their heads were on the block along with the soviets. But it was a sign of things to come.

From now until October there would be more trials of the masses' patience and the Bolsheviks' ability to steer their activity to the final goal of workers' power. The "April Days" crisis resulted in a new coalition government which included Menshevik and SR representatives. On 1 May, the moderate Executive Committee (Exec Com) of the Petrograd Soviet voted 44 to 19 (12 Bolsheviks, three Menshevik-Internationalists, four SRs) with two abstentions, for their participation. The masses of workers and soldiers thought this was a way of crowding out the bourgeoisie, an illusion fostered by the Menshevik paper, *Rabochaia Gazeta*: "The provisional government cut itself off completely from imperialist influences. And it quite definitely enters upon the road for the most rapid achievement of universal peace through international means".[66]

Nothing could have been further from the truth. The enthusiasm of supporters of the war was given a boost. On 6 May, *Izvestiia*, the daily paper of the Soviet Exec Com brazenly addressed the soldiers, thinking that they had found the arguments they needed to legitimise the war:

> the soldier may now believe that all military operations are equally serving one and the same goal – the defence of the revolution from destruction and the earliest possible conclusion of universal peace. From now on, they can and must accomplish their military feats in the firm belief that they are acting for a national cause, for the cause of the workers of the whole world.[67]

The first trial of strength

The government ordered a military offensive in June. This and calls by supporters of the war to send troops from Petrograd to the front had the soldiers in ferment. Agitation by the Bolsheviks' Military Organisation for protest action backed up by unrest among factory workers put Lenin's position of "patiently explain" under pressure. Rather than talk, the most militant Bolshevik workers and soldiers wanted *action*. The Bolsheviks resolved to call a demonstration for Saturday, 10 June. Among the slogans to be raised were: "All Power to the All-Russian Soviet of Workers' and Soldiers' Deputies!", "Time to end the war! Let the Soviet of Deputies declare just conditions of peace!" and "Bread! Peace! Liberty!".

The protest would raise the rights of the soldiers – established in February, but now being rolled back – would challenge the growing number of lock-outs of workers by bosses, and raise the question of workers' control of industry. The Soviet Exec Com, however, banned the demonstration. In the Bolsheviks' own ranks, the Petrograd Soviet delegates were swelled by the presence of representatives from the provinces away from the city hotbeds. They reflected the more hesitant atmosphere that prevailed in the countryside and were pressuring the Central Committee (CC) to call off the banned demonstration. Under immense pressure on all sides the Bolshevik CC literally at the last moment – in the early hours of the morning of the 10th – called it off, with Lenin abstaining. Numerous factory committees censured the CC, and resentment at this retreat was widespread. But the moderate Soviet leadership, confident they had dealt a serious blow to the Bolsheviks, instead handed them a victory. An official demonstration was called for Sunday 18 June. Tsereteli, Menshevik leader of the Soviet, addressed the Bolsheviks in a triumphant speech: "Now we shall all see which the majority follows, you or us. This isn't a matter of underhand plots but a duel in the open arena. Tomorrow we shall see".[68]

And see they did. The Bolshevik leaders urged their supporters to organise "a demonstration within a demonstration", to come with the slogans planned for 10 June and more. They had to overcome a reluctance by some of their most impatient and militant members to participate in an official demonstration that was replacing their own. The leadership called for unions, factories, military units to mobilise. And they did mobilise – 400,000 marched. Miliukov admitted in his memoirs that the demonstration "showed again that in Petrograd undoubtedly the Bolshevik slogans and mood predominated and that even in a demonstration friendly to the government to speak of support for the coalition government was simply impossible".[69] Sukhanov, no sympathiser of the Bolsheviks, included this account in his memoirs:

> The masses had been called and they had come … Probably some felt that they were doing not their own business but something compulsory … There was a businesslike veneer … But it was on a magnificent scale. All worker and soldier Petersburg took part in it.
>
> But what was the political character of the demonstration?
>
> "All Power to the Soviets!" "Down with the Ten Capitalist Ministers!" "Peace for the hovels, war for the palaces!"
>
> In this sturdy and weighty way worker-peasant Petersburg, the vanguard of the Russian and the world revolution, expressed its will. The situation

was absolutely unambiguous. Here and there the chain of Bolshevik flags and columns was interrupted by specifically SR and official Soviet slogans. But they were submerged in the mass; they seemed to be exceptions, intentionally confirming the rule. Again and again, like the unchanging summons of the very depths of the revolutionary capital, like fate itself... there advanced toward us: "All Power to the Soviets!" "Down with the Ten Capitalist Ministers!"

I remembered the purblind Tsereteli's fervour of the night before. Here was the duel in the open arena! Here was the honest legal review of forces in an official Soviet Demonstration![70]

The July Days: an opening for the counter-revolution

All through June pressure was building in Petrograd for an armed uprising to transfer power from the government to the soviets. Fuelling this ferment were provocations by the government. The day after the 18 June demonstration, soldiers were sent to evict anarchists who had occupied the Durnovo Villa. Workers in the area rallied to defend them, and the anarchists used the confrontation and the death of one of their members to agitate for an armed show of strength. At the same time Kerensky, the new minister of war, had ordered an offensive by the army on the front, fuelling calls by the Kronstadt garrison and the First Machine Gun Regiment for an armed demonstration against the government. Some soldiers began touring the factories, agitating for support:

> [O]n the Vyborg side factories stopped operating as soon as trucks bearing the machine gunners appeared, and workers in many of them scurried for their weapons almost immediately. Something like ten thousand in the Putilov factory were soon to follow suit.[71]

But Lenin still insisted that to achieve the Petrograd masses' desire for a Soviet government, the other industrial cities had to be convinced and more conscious of what was at stake, and the peasantry had to be mobilised into self-activity and a greater awareness of the need to transfer power. They had to understand that their demands would never be met by the provisional government. This could only be achieved by a combination of experience and discussion. The role of the Bolsheviks and the militants close to them had to be to convince wider layers to continue patiently explaining, exposing every counter-revolutionary move by the government and its backers, urging the masses to prepare to take things into their own hands.

In the end the Bolsheviks could not restrain the militants. Some of their own agitators gave the impression they supported an uprising. So Lenin accepted that in order to minimise the danger, they would have to participate, not to overthrow the government, but to ensure there was no such attempt.[72] Beginning on 3 July, hundreds of thousands of workers and soldiers participated in armed demonstrations, some involving clashes with counter-revolutionary gangs. On the 7th, the Bolsheviks called for a retreat, for which they suffered scathing attacks from militants, including some of their own members, for lack of leadership and determination.

Immediately, a witch hunt against the Bolsheviks was launched. The government and its supporters thought their chance to destroy the Bolsheviks once and for all had come. They trotted out every lie and slander they could dredge up, including the ludicrous allegation that Lenin and other leading Bolsheviks were agents in the service of the German high command. They used the fact that Lenin and others had returned to Russia through Germany on a "sealed train" by arrangement with the German government. It was irrelevant that other, more moderate socialists such as Martov had followed once the Bolsheviks showed it could be done. The point wasn't the truth, but an opportunity to cause as much doubt and confusion in the ranks of the workers and soldiers as possible. These were revolutionaries who had lived their lives often in exile, in jail, hounded by governments around Europe, who had urged workers of all countries to turn their guns on their own rulers, and who staked the future of the Russian workers' struggles on a successful revolution in Germany in particular. More seriously, the slander that the Bolsheviks deliberately tried to stage an insurrection in early

July which is accepted as standard wisdom among many historians was established during this campaign of lies against the Bolsheviks. The motives of the counter-revolution are clear – discredit the Bolsheviks to demoralise the masses – but the propagation of later historians continues in the face of overwhelming evidence to the contrary. Lenin's arguments in the last days of June, falling on the heads of the militants like hammer blows, remain as forceful today as when they were penned:

> We must be especially attentive and careful, so as not to be drawn into a provocation... One wrong move on our part can wreck everything... If we were now able to seize power, it is naive to think that having taken it we would be able to hold it...
>
> What is the exact weight of our fraction in the Soviet? Even in the Soviets of both capitals, not to speak now of the others, we are an insignificant minority. And what does this fact show? It cannot be brushed aside. It shows that the majority of the masses are wavering but still believe the SRs and Mensheviks...
>
> In order to gain power seriously (not by Blanquist methods), the proletarian party must fight for influence inside the Soviet, patiently, unswervingly, explaining to the masses from day to day the error of their petty-bourgeois illusions...
>
> Events should not be anticipated. Time is on our side.[73]

This was the theme running through Lenin's speeches and articles. Not that it was enthusiastically received by the militants in his own party. A participant in the Bolshevik military conference on 20 June recalled:

> [T]he spirit prevailing in some party circles to the effect that there was no point in waiting, that it was now time to seize power. Lenin came out hotly and sharply against such views. For a large part of the conference his views were received with disappointment or even dissatisfaction.

Another remembered that Lenin's speech was like a "cold shower" for the "hotheads". The myth that Lenin initiated an insurrection is convenient for those who portray October as nothing more than a coup, because it "proves" that Lenin wasn't interested in *workers'* power, only power for himself. Richard Pipes argues that Lenin orchestrated an attempted "putsch", but the Bolsheviks had to retreat when they realised it would fail. Whereas Lenin's arguments in July and October, when contrasted, make it crystal clear that he was for an insurrection with the backing of the vast majority of the oppressed so that the soviets could take power.[74]

A textbook used in high schools in Australia simply comments that Trotsky "claimed" that "the movement had begun...against their will". In so far as it is accepted this might be true, it is attributed to a narrow concern with the Bolsheviks' own fortunes: "[T]hey did not want power to fall into the hands of the Socialist Revolutionaries and Mensheviks, who at this time dominated the Petrograd Soviet". Of course Lenin didn't want power to fall into the hands of those moderates who were sitting in the government. His whole, very public, argument was that they needed to be overthrown! His argument was that if the moderates could still command a majority in the soviets, then this showed that the mass of workers and soldiers were not clear that they had to be overthrown and so any attempt at an insurrection would be defeated.

Miliukov, who had been replaced as foreign minister in the provisional government by then, is the only authority invoked by the authors of the textbook for their unimaginative argument. Miliukov explains the uprising as an experiment by the Bolsheviks from which they learnt how difficult it would be to get power. They would prepare more systematically next time. But Lenin understood the difficulties *before* the July days; they just confirmed his opinions. Miliukov does admit that "the winners [the counter-revolutionaries] took their rapid victory too lightly and by no means appreciated the importance of those factors whose effect had caused them several unpleasant hours". Not one reference in the textbook to the repeated arguments Lenin made both to the hotheads in his own party, and to the impatient soldiers and workers who wanted to take on the government once and for all finds its way into a text for the "education" of the youth of today.[75]

This is not simply a historical debate about the integrity or intentions of the Bolsheviks. The different accounts of the July Days reflect fundamentally different attitudes to revolution. The only way to understand the July Days is in the context of dual power and the need for workers to take power through the soviets. The view that the Bolsheviks attempted a coup flows from a hatred of the very conception of workers taking power, or a disbelief that workers are capable of such political action on their own behalf. Usually both prejudices are entwined.

In July and August 1917, the opponents of workers' power such as the landlords, the generals and the capitalists saw the premature uprising as the opening Lenin knew it would present them. And they grasped that opportunity with fervour. The Bolshevik presses were smashed, and the party leaders jailed. Lenin firmly believed he and other leaders were likely to be shot, and so rather than answer his accusers as to whether he was a German agent or not, went into hiding. This was not some hysterical posture, but flowed from an assessment of the actual situation of the balance of power and the goal of the counter-revolution. The Bolshevik leaders weren't shot in this instance, but how well Lenin understood the possibilities is demonstrated by the fact that in a similar situation in Germany in January 1919, Rosa Luxemburg and Karl Liebknecht, the two great leaders of the revolution, were killed by soldiers under the command of the Social Democratic Party, the party that played the same role as the fake socialists in Russia.

State and Revolution

The difference between 1917 in Russia and eighteen months later in Germany was the existence of Lenin's Bolshevik Party, painstakingly built over years in preparation for the revolution, and the absence of such an experienced party in Germany. The July Days of 1917 illuminate like a spotlight the need for such a party. No revolution is carried through by a uniformly radicalised and experienced working class, to say nothing of the middle classes who surround them. As in all revolutions, the spontaneous actions of masses of workers put new political problems on the agenda. As Trotsky says:

> A revolution teaches and teaches fast. In that lies its strength. Every week brings something new to the masses. Every two months creates an epoch. At the end of February, the insurrection. At the end of April, a demonstration of the armed workers and soldiers in Petrograd. At the beginning of July, a new assault, far broader in scope and under more resolute slogans.[76]

The first flush of success, when the state seems incapable of withstanding the hammer blows of the working class, creates an atmosphere of unity. Even the rich pretend that they are for social change, for they dare not show their true colours. But in the standoff of dual power, they can wait for their opening to reassert their former power. It was during 1917 that Lenin wrote his book *State and Revolution*, in which he restated Marx's understanding that the working class needed to entirely destroy the capitalist state and to replace it with their own workers' state based on workers' organisations of mass democracy.

The conflict between the provisional government and the soviets could only be resolved by the complete victory of one or the other, because the exploiters cannot share power with those they exploit. You only have to remember the way they railed against the influence of the soviets, and their demands for an end to this dual power to see how clear they were about that. In the coming months we will see their determination to regain complete control.

But masses of newly radicalised workers and soldiers did not clearly see what was at stake. They hoped there could be a settlement that would include all the parties that had participated in the February Revolution. Others, awakening to the immensity of the road ahead, were impatient. The middle classes and the vast peasant masses were left straggling behind. And Lenin understood that if power was to be transferred to the soviets as increasing numbers demanded, those who lagged behind had to be brought up to the level of the most advanced. The workers and soldiers in one or two industrial centres would not be able to hold onto power unless they took the whole country with them. And July clearly demonstrated the danger of impatience and premature action.

There had been hints of the danger posed by the counter-revolution and the treacherous role of the moderate socialists, but they had only confused many workers. On 11 June an assembly of the Soviet Exec Com and leaders of the various factions, numbering a hundred, met to discuss the abandoned Bolshevik demonstration. Tsereteli, a leading Menshevik and leader of the Soviet, angrily accused the Bolsheviks of a conspiracy and demanded "We have got to disarm the Bolsheviks". But what did this mean? Sukhanov comments:

> The Bolsheviks really did not have any special stores of weapons. All the weapons were actually in the hands of soldiers and workers, the immense mass of whom were following the Bolsheviks. Disarming the Bolsheviks could mean only disarming the proletariat. More than that, it meant disarming the troops.[77]

And Trotsky sums up:

> In other words, that classic moment of the revolution had arrived when the bourgeois democracy, upon the demand of the reaction, undertakes to disarm the workers who had guaranteed the revolutionary victory. These democratic gentlemen, among whom were well-read people, had invariably given their sympathy to the disarmed, not to the disarmers – so long as it was a question of reading old books... The mere fact that Tsereteli, a revolutionist, a man who had spent years at hard labour...was undertaking to disarm the workers, had some difficulty in making its way into people's heads. The hall was stunned into silence. The delegates nevertheless felt that someone was pushing them into an abyss.

The mass demonstration on 18 June that ended as a show of Bolshevik strength and mass support for the slogan "All power to the soviets!" gave a boost to the expectations and impatience of the most militant workers and soldiers. Surely the majority were with them? In this situation, if they had not had years of experience and the substantial authority they gained in those years, the Bolsheviks would not have been able to prevent a premature confrontation. And such an outcome could well have handed power to the capitalists and their reactionary backers. An organisation that could withstand serious disagreements, which had the authority and the nerve to see the period of unpopularity through and survive such a crisis intact could only be built over long years of struggle. Even the "epochs" of Trotsky's revolutionary calendar could not steel the necessary organisation. The failure of a newly formed, but revolutionary, Communist Party in Germany in 1919 was a tragic confirmation of the correctness of Lenin's unswerving work *before* 1917 to build his party.

The campaign to discredit the Bolsheviks was not aimed at clarifying reality and the prospects for a favourable end to the workers' struggles, but was an escalation of the counter-revolutionary forces to ensure a favourable outcome for the capitalists and their hangers-on. And for a few weeks the Bolsheviks seemed to be hounded on all sides, with their leadership either in hiding or in jail. However, as Lenin had insisted, time was on the Bolsheviks' side. Their enemies could not be content with a witch hunt against the revolutionaries. They had to smash the power of the workers' and soldiers' soviets. Any move to do this would begin to clarify the reality of dual power.

The counter-revolution comes out of the shadows

Guchkov, the war minister, had said after the crisis created by Miliukov's note to the Allies about continuing the war back in April:

> [T]he country cannot exist under conditions of dual power... The pernicious slogan..."Peace on the front, and war at home" – this preaching of international peace at any price, and of civil war at any cost – this slogan must be drowned by the imperative call of the Great Russian Nation. "War on the front, peace at home".[78]

After the July Days the full meaning of Guchkov's proclamation began to emerge into full view. Not only were the Bolsheviks subject to repression, the government ordered that regiments and battalions that had participated in the July Days be disbanded. General Kornilov, general commander of the south-western front, ordered that retreating soldiers be fired on with machine guns and artillery, and the death penalty was restored at the front.

Employers were sabotaging production, increasing the suffering and sense of crisis caused by growing hunger and destitution in the war-ravaged economy. On the other hand, they were increasingly challenging the elements of workers' control over production exercised by the factory committees. In June a circular from the minister of labour made veiled threats to those "workers [who] often refuse to negotiate with employers and insist, under threat of violence, on the satisfaction of their demands".

> With full freedom to organise, it cannot be tolerated that conscientious workers who resort to such methods are employed in enterprises that produce articles of prime necessity to the State and, especially, in the railroads, the situation assumes the aspect of a direct threat to the gains of the revolution.[79]

The aim behind the circular was more clearly exposed in the editorial in *Ruskiia Vedomosti*, the daily newspaper of the liberal capitalists:

> [C]onsiderable peace of mind will come from the assurance of the minister that "the provisional government sets for itself the task of doing all in its power to combat the economic disorganisation." One of the methods in this struggle will be government control of industries – a measure that is desirable, timely, and necessary, the more so that it opposes the advocacy of seizing enterprises by workers themselves.

Managers orchestrated a massive campaign of factory lockouts and suppression of factory committees. And the Congress of Trade and Industry, the main organisation of the capitalists, stepped up their demands to dissolve the workers' and soldiers' soviets. In the provinces, land committees were arrested *en masse*. John Reed, in his famous account of these months, recounts how businessmen spoke of winter as "always Russia's best friend. Perhaps now it will rid us of revolution". He wrote that "the secretary of the Petrograd branch of the Cadet party told me that the break-down of the country's economic life was part of a campaign to discredit the Revolution".

> An Allied diplomat...confirmed this from his own knowledge. I know of certain coal mines near Kharkov which were fired and flooded by their owners, of textile factories at Moscow whose engineers put the machinery out of order when they left, or railroad officials caught by the workers in the act of crippling locomotives.[80]

As the Bolsheviks predicted, the reactionaries were teaching the workers what the real situation was. On 28 August a factory committee published a letter of protest which said in part:

> [W]e are forced to state that the Ministry for the "protection of labour" has a matter of fact been converted in to a Ministry for the protection of capitalist interests, and acts hand in hand with [capitalists] in order to reduce the country to famine so that the "bony hand" may strangle the Russian revolution.[81]

Increasingly the question was posed: who was going to control the production of wealth in Russia? As one recorder of events described the situation:

> Under the double influence of political events (kornilovshina, the unavoidable crises of coalition government, delay and vacillations in the struggle for peace) and the aggravated economic disintegration and the change to the offensive by capital (sabotage and concealed lockouts), a spontaneous move toward the left was taking place inside the working class and in the trade union organisations, which could not but be felt... The October Revolution was approaching.[82]

Guchkov outlines in his memoirs how he and other reactionaries began to deal with the situation:

[A] private committee, consisting of banks and insurance companies, was organised at the initiative of AI Putilov [owner of the biggest factory in Russia, the Putilov steel works]. I, too, joined this committee. In order to give an official justification for our existence, we called ourselves the Society for the Economic Rehabilitation of Russia. Actually, we set for ourselves the aim of establishing a large fund for supporting moderate bourgeois candidates to the Constituent Assembly and for combating the influence of socialists at the front. In the end, we decided to place the large funds that we collected at the disposal of General Kornilov for the purposes of organising an armed struggle against the Soviets.[83]

Increasingly the bourgeoisie and the government that defended their interests came to support a military assault on Petrograd to end the power of the soviets once and for all. Leave aside that who was to wage that attack was an open question, their hypocrisy knew no bounds. While the vile slander campaign against the Bolsheviks was whipping up hysteria against the "traitors", bourgeois figures were ever more openly admitting that they preferred a German takeover to the continued power of the soviets. Rodzianko, a former chairman of the Duma wrote:

> Petrograd is in danger. I say to myself, "Let God take care of Petrograd." They fear that if Petrograd is lost the central revolutionary organisations will be destroyed. To that I answer that I rejoice if all these organisations are destroyed; for they will bring nothing but disaster upon Russia...
>
> With the taking of Petrograd, the Baltic fleet will also be destroyed ... But there will be nothing to regret.[84]

John Reed wrote that his experience was that

> a large section of the propertied classes preferred the Germans to the Revolution – even to the provisional government – and didn't hesitate to say so. In the Russian household where I lived, the subject of conversation at the dinner table was almost invariably the coming of the Germans, bringing "law and order".

When a Moscow merchant asked eleven people at a dinner party who they preferred, "Wilhelm or the Bolsheviki", the vote was ten to one for Wilhelm.[85]

At first, Kerensky, as head of the provisional government, cooperated with Kornilov, who was planning a coup to instigate a military dictatorship. But, as Sukhanov noted, Kerensky "was a Kornolovite – on condition that he himself head the Kornilov rising". Gradually Kerensky came to understand this would not be the outcome of his support for Kornilov's advancing attack on Petrograd, and he turned against him. On 27 August in a national proclamation Kerensky told the nation that Kornilov had demanded the surrender by the provisional government of all civil and military power: "I am taking all necessary measures to protect the liberty and order of the country, and the population will be informed in due time with regard to such measures".[86]

A united front to defend the revolution

But Kerensky patently could not mobilise the masses to defend the revolution against his recent co-conspirator. That task fell to the Bolsheviks, the only organisation in the whole of Russia that stood on the basis of clear principle and honesty, the only party dedicated to the victory of the working class. Semi-legal, persecuted by Kerensky, its leaders slandered and jailed, you might think they would be inclined to stand back and watch the demise of their persecutor. But Lenin was adamant: defend the Kerensky government from a military coup, but no political support for it. And the way to defeat Kornilov was by revolutionary means: arm the working class, mobilise the masses and use their power as workers to thwart this mortal threat to the revolution:

> We shall fight, we are fighting against Kornilov, just as Kerensky's troops do, but we do not support Kerensky. On the contrary, we expose his weakness. There is the difference...

> We must say: now is the time for action; you SR and Menshevik gentlemen have long since worn these phrases threadbare. Now is the time for action; the war against Kornilov must be conducted in a revolutionary way, by

drawing the masses in, by arousing them, by inflaming them (Kerensky is afraid of the masses, afraid of the people).[87]

As Sukhanov observed:

> At that time, [the Bolshevik Party] was the only organisation that was large, welded together by elementary discipline, and united with the democratic rank and file of the capital. Without them the Military Revolutionary Committee was impotent... With the Bolsheviks...the Military Revolutionary Committee had at its disposal all organised worker-soldier strength, of whatever kind.[88]

The effect of Kornilov's march on Petrograd was to galvanise masses of people into action, transforming the situation:

> The news of Kornilov's march on Petrograd broke on the working-class districts on the night of 27–28 August in an atmosphere of pent up rage and frustration... [T]he workers' response was far from panic. In fact the howl of the factory horns announcing the emergency seemed to dispel in one swoop the sluggish, depressed mood of the preceding two months. There followed a show of enthusiasm, the like of which had not been seen since February.[89]

Under the leadership of the Bolsheviks, the factory committees of Petrograd organised detachments of Red Guards made up mostly of Bolsheviks and numbering as many as 40,000. A gunpowder works sent a load of grenades for distribution to workers, and the Putilov steel works became a centre of resistance, working 16 hours a day to produce 100 cannon. Unarmed workers formed companies for trench digging, sheet-metal fortification, barbed wire fencing. The railroad workers used their control over transport to divert troops from their destinations and to send artillery to the wrong places; they even tore up the tracks in some strategic places. The telegraphers kept the workers informed of Kornilov's troop movements, and held up his communications. Information intended for Kornilov often ended up pasted up as posters around the city for all to read.

As Trotsky says: "The generals had been accustomed...to think of transport and communications as technical questions. They found out now that these were political questions". The coup collapsed in four days. "The insurrection had rolled back, crumbled to pieces, been sucked up by the earth" wrote Trotsky in his *History*.[90] And an important lesson in revolutionary strategy was established: how to form a united front with forces who in the long run have to be discredited and defeated in order to defend the interests of the working class.

However, the provisional government remained a reactionary one, and the SRs and Mensheviks continued to give it support. On 3 September, Kerensky, in his new position of supreme commander (having replaced Kornilov), issued an order to the army and navy with General Alekseev, former chief of staff under the tsar and now back in that position: "For the restoration of order I command: the cessation of all political struggle among the troops... The discontinuation immediately of the arbitrary formation of detachments under the pretext of combating counter-revolutionary action".

And only authorities under his control were permitted to carry out arrests of officers under suspicion, a direct attack on the political rights that the soldiers' committees had established. The uproar was immediate, even Menshevik publications voicing disquiet.[91]

The struggle had taken a giant step forward, but had not reached its destiny. And the importance of that step forward was the light it cast on the situation for the mass of workers and soldiers. As Lenin argued in a different context:

> [T]he great significance of all crises is that they unveil the hidden, cast aside the conventional, the superficial, the petty, sweep away the political rubbish, uncover the secret springs of the true class struggle that is going on.[92]

Chapter five
October: the workers take power

LENIN'S WRITINGS DURING SEPTEMBER AND EARLY OCTOBER are some of his most inspiring. He passionately delineates the revolutionary approach to the struggle for workers' power. His arguments make it absolutely clear that, contrary to his detractors' claims, he had no intention of the Bolsheviks seizing power for the sake of their own factional interests. Again and again, he lays out that it is the masses who will rule. The Bolsheviks, now a quarter of a million members, represent the most advanced, class-conscious and determined workers, and they can now, unlike in July, expect to carry the broad mass of workers, soldiers and poor peasants with them. The final blow that defeated bourgeois power was the culmination of developing class consciousness among the masses, and a decisive act in the unfolding class struggle. Before the experience of the Kornilov revolt, the workers and soldiers would not have defended a new government. But now they could understand the role of the compromising "socialists", and of the provisional government:

> An insurrection on 3–4 July would have been a mistake; we could not have retained power either physically or politically...because our workers and soldiers would not have *fought and died* for Petrograd. There was not at the time that "savageness", or fierce hatred *both* of the Kerenskys *and of* the Tseretelis and Chernovs. Our people had still not been tempered by the experience of the persecution of the Bolsheviks in which the Socialist Revolutionaries and Mensheviks participated.[93]

Lenin understood that the moment when workers would trust them, when they were confident to take power, would ebb away if it appeared as if yet another party they looked to could do nothing but prevaricate.

The danger was the mass of workers and soldiers would retreat into the struggle for individual survival and their revolutionary consciousness would subside, leaving the way open for a final, and possibly successful blow from the likes of Kornilov:

> in order for an insurrection to be crowned with success it should have the support, not of a conspiracy, not of a party, but of the advanced class; that first of all. The insurrection must rest on a popular revolutionary upsurge: that is second. The insurrection must come at the historic turning point of the expanding revolution, at the moment when the activity of the masses reaches its peak, and when the hesitation in the ranks of the enemy, and among the false friends of the revolution, the double-dealers and the faint hearts, reaches its peak. That is third. By thus posing the three conditions of insurrection, Marxism distinguishes itself from Blanquism.[94]

He linked the fate of the Russian working class and its revolution with that of the world socialist revolution. They could not build socialism in Russia alone – no country could build socialism in isolation – but in backward Russia, it was even more urgent that they get the support they would need from the proletariat of Germany and the rest of the most advanced capitalist world. This will become a crucial question after October. But first, Lenin had to wage a bitter fight against the leaders of his own party such as Zinoviev and Kamenev. Again and again, he returned to the urgent need to transfer power to the soviets.

Historians like to point to the lack of mass mobilisations as "proof" that October was a coup carried out by the Bolsheviks in isolation from the masses.[95] There was no need for the masses to march in the streets calling for "all power to the soviets"; the soviets were already running most of society and the majority of the army had been won to support for the transfer of power to the soviets. These trends were expressed in the Baltic fleet and among the soldiers' sections of the soviets. Peasant committees were beginning to organise the seizure of the landlords' estates. These facts were of critical significance to Lenin because they indicated that an insurrection could count on the support it would need to succeed. And Sukhanov says "After the

Kornilov revolt, Bolshevism began blossoming luxuriantly and put forth deep roots throughout the country".[96] This was not a constitutional or formal question for Lenin. It was not just a question of factional advantage over the Bolsheviks' rivals, but an important indicator of mass consciousness.

But Lenin had to continue arguing inside the Bolsheviks about how to maximise this rising level of consciousness. In agitated notes sent to the Bolsheviks from his hiding place, he attacked the Bolshevik fraction for their compromising role in what was known as the Democratic Conference in mid-September. The fake socialists were doing all they could to use the conference to lull the workers and soldiers into a false sense of security, and to create an aura of consensus to dispel the atmosphere of crisis after the Kornilov threat. Lenin was clear as to where the Bolsheviks should have their sights at this most critical juncture:

> The Bolsheviks should have walked out of the meeting in protest and not allowed themselves to be caught by the conference trap set to divert the people's attention from serious questions. The Bolsheviks should have left two or three of their 136 delegates for "liaison" work, that is, to report by telephone the moment the idiotic babbling came to an end and the voting began. They should not have allowed themselves to be kept busy with obvious nonsense for the obvious purpose of deceiving the people with the obvious aim of extinguishing the growing revolution by wasting time on trivial matters.
>
> Ninety-nine percent of the Bolshevik delegation ought to have gone to the factories and barracks; that was the proper place for delegates who had come from all ends of Russia and who...could see the full depth of the Socialist Revolutionary and Menshevik rottenness. There, closer to the masses, at hundreds and thousands of meetings and talks, they ought to have discussed the lessons of this farcical conference...
>
> Parliamentarism should be used, especially in revolutionary times, not to waste valuable time over representatives of what is rotten, but to use the example of what is rotten to teach the masses.[97]

The insurrection

Wednesday 25 October is the day the revolution is celebrated, but by then the government had to all intents and purposes been overthrown. This is a fact ignored by all those who accuse the Bolsheviks of carrying out a coup behind the backs of the masses. They do not understand the insurrection as the culmination of mass preparations for a transfer of power that were taking place for at least the three weeks leading up to the 25th. For instance, the school textbook *The Spirit of Change* narrates the events of 1917 honestly, looking at how Bolshevik influence grew not just because of their clever propaganda, but because of the counter-revolution and Kornilov's attempted coup. But under the heading "How did the Bolsheviks seize power?" they refer to October as a "Bolshevik revolution" and look only at a resolution passed by the Petrograd garrison and the attempt by Polkovnikov to discipline the rebellious soldiers on 24 October.[98] Another popular textbook gives the accurate assessment that historians think October was a coup or a popular revolution depending on whether they oppose or support Communism. Nevertheless, they too deal with October by beginning with 24 October, and present it as a military exercise by the Bolsheviks, directing units of soldiers to the appropriate places.[99] To a large extent this is a fair account – if you begin with 24 October.

However, if we look at the weeks prior to 24 October, the picture is dramatically different. It highlights the mass involvement in preparations to take power, the incredible wave of organising that swept the propertied classes from power. Trotsky gives a rich and inspiring account of the mobilisation for the insurrection. But we do not have to rely on him. Historian Alexander Rabinowitch, who gained access to many Russian archives nearly four decades after Trotsky wrote his epic, produced a narrative that endorses Trotsky on every count.[100]

Let's begin with a famous meeting of the Bolshevik Central Committee on 10 October. It decided the approaching Congress of Soviets should seize power and this meant insurrection. Kamenev and Zinoviev publicly disavowed this decision, so there ensued a very public debate over whether the Bolsheviks should initiate an insurrectionary uprising. The Northern Regional Congress of Soviets was meeting at the time and Lenin was agitating for that Congress to take action, afraid that the moment was passing. But many of the Bolsheviks concluded from this Congress that it was not possible to take and hold power. However it was a turning point in the advance towards the resolution of the intolerable situation of dual power. Rabinowitch found that "[a]s it turned out, the Northern Region Congress was for the most part a thundering, highly visible expression of ultra-radical sentiment".[101]

After this there was a growing crescendo of reactionary and moderate "socialist" papers condemning the Bolsheviks for agitating for an uprising. With Lenin in hiding, Trotsky was in effect leading the Bolsheviks. He supported Lenin's appeals for an insurrection, but he differed on the tactics of how the transfer of power could successfully be carried out. He was playing for time and organising, with his eyes firmly fixed on the coming Congress of the Soviet of Workers' and Soldiers' Deputies.

On 14 October, when Dan, a Menshevik, demanded to know if the Bolsheviks were calling on the workers to "come out", Riazanov's reply to the All-Russian Exec Com meeting was "we demand peace and land". In the event, it was a provocation by the provisional government that began the final round of mobilisation, just as Trotsky anticipated. In the second week of October, the government suddenly announced plans to move the Petrograd garrison to the front, contrary to every understanding by the masses since February. Rabinowitch catalogues the reaction: "Soldiers in Petrograd reacted to news of these orders with predictable vehemence. In unison, garrison troops proclaimed their lack of confidence in the provisional government and demanded the transfer of power to the soviets...".

He speaks of an "avalanche of antigovernment resolutions adopted by garrison units". For a week Petrograd was a hothouse of mass meetings, not just in the barracks but also in the factories. The streets were swamped by papers debating the latest moves. At the instigation of the Bolsheviks, on 15 October soldiers were dispatched to the front to explain the political reasons for the garrison's refusal to provide relief: they did not trust the motives of the provisional government, not that they wanted to avoid their responsibilities. This move led to a conference of delegates from the front and the city garrison including representatives from the soviets. To the frustration of generals and the moderate socialists, at this conference on 17 October,

> the discussion was concerned as much with the need for transfer of power to the soviets, for peace, and for the long-suffering front-line soldier to return home, as it was with the question of getting new regiments into the trenches.[102]

On 18 October, the soldiers held a garrison conference and endorsed their hostility to the government and a call for the transfer of power to the soviets. This was not to say that they supported an uprising, but they would support any actions necessary to defend the soviets from the government and other reactionaries.

But the date which is of great significance is Sunday the 22nd, Petrograd Soviet Day. Not that you would know that anything happened on that day from historians such as Orlando Figes.[103] The Bolsheviks saw it as a means to assess the balance of class forces and the preparedness of the masses for the insurrection. Concerts, speech-making, mass meetings in factories around the city, massive gatherings in the streets and in public halls from morning till night where old and young, women, men and children, stood patiently for hours soaking up the words of orators such as Trotsky, Volodarsky, Lashevich, Alexandra Kollantai, Raskolnikov and Krylenko. One typical such meeting was in the House of the People: "Well before the start of the program a massive crowd of factory workers, soldiers, and a smattering of lower-middle-class townspeople filled the colossal opera house, primarily to see and hear the legendary Trotsky".

Trotsky summed up the Bolsheviks' main points: that the government was preparing to surrender Petrograd to the Germans rather than allow the soviets to rule, that the entire world would be engulfed by revolution if they took power, and that only a soviet regime could bring peace, distribute the land and defend true democracy. A journalist reported that when asked for a pledge of support for the soviet when it moved from words to deeds, the huge audience threw up its hands and chanted "We swear it!". And Sukhanov, another of Trotsky's audience, wrote also of Trotsky's appeals for a vow to carry through the revolution: "The vast crowd was holding up its hands. It agreed. It vowed..."[104]

Three days earlier, Trotsky had won a serious victory at a mass meeting of soldiers at the Peter and Paul Fortress, a strategically important military centre. A huge mass meeting in the fortress square went on for hours, even after Trotsky spoke. But when it came to it, the overwhelming majority voted that military orders should only be obeyed from the Military Revolutionary Committee. "Remaining in opposition to the Military Revolutionary Committee was a small group of officers and intellectuals among the cyclists [one of the most reactionary sections of the soldiers]."[105]

Alongside all of these activities, the Red Guards continued to drill, to be tutored in handling of arms, patrolled factories and streets, preparing to defend a soviet takeover. As Trotsky outlines, the whole situation was leading inexorably to rule by the working class not just in the main cities, but also in the provinces:

> In the provincial industrial regions...armed workers would remove managers and engineers, and even arrest them. In the Urals...companies of Red Guards led by the old veterans established law and order. Armed workers almost unnoticeably dissolved the old government and replaced it with soviet institutions. Sabotage on the part of the property owners and administrators shifted to the workers the task of protecting the plants... Roles were here interchanged: the worker would tightly grip his rifle in defence of the factory in which he saw the source of his power. In this way elements of a workers' dictatorship were inaugurated in the factories and districts some time before the proletariat as a whole seized the state power.[106]

In Petrograd, where the leadership of the provisional government and the influence of the compromising socialists was greatest, the Red Guards could not impose their will so easily. However, Trotsky argues "the Kornilov insurrection conclusively legalised the Red Guard". About 25,000 workers were at least partially armed and being drilled. One worker recalled that now they drilled openly in parks and on the boulevards instead of in their homes. Another says of October "the shops [meaning workplaces] were turned into camps... The worker would stand at his bench with knapsack on his back and rifle beside him". From 10 October, with insurrection openly on the agenda, the Red Guards enrolled virtually every worker in some factories. The commanding staff were all elected. All were volunteers and knew each other, so this was a new form of military organisation emerging out of the revolutionary process.

Working women created Red Cross divisions, organised lectures on the care of the wounded and in the factories were organised as bands of nurses. On 24 October, the Vyborg district Soviet issued an order to "immediately requisition all automobiles... Take an inventory of all first-aid supplies, and have nurses on duty in all clinics". And all the time, the Red Guards and other organisations were drawing in increasing numbers of non-Bolshevik workers. Bolshevik workers were surprised and pleased to find Menshevik and Socialist Revolutionary workers joining in the activity "and even developing some initiative", says the Bolshevik Tatiana Graff.[107] And on 22 October the Red Guards also held a mass conference to finalise their plans for the insurrection.

Moscow was moving to soviet power as well. In response to a wave of strikes, a factory committee initiated an idea the Bolsheviks took up: a plan to settle economic conflicts. The result was "Revolutionary Decree No. 1" adopted by the soviets. Workers and clerks in factories and shops would henceforth be employed or discharged only with the consent of the shop committees. As Trotsky says, "this meant that the soviet had begun to function as a state power".[108]

While the masses were mobilising, the government was increasingly isolated and paralysed. Trotsky says that in the final confrontation, "the weakness of the government exceeded all expectation". Miliukov himself, Cadet and head of the provisional government, admits that "the government proved weaker than [even Trotsky] expected, and the power fell into his [Trotsky's] hands of its own accord". And every effort by the government to shore up its position was interpreted by the workers and soldiers as the act of aggression it was.

The raising of the bridges [by the government] was received by the population as an official announcement of the beginning of the insurrection... [The] struggle for the bridges assumed the character of a test for both sides... Only Dvortsovy Bridge remained several hours in the hands of the government patrols.[109]

At 5.30am on 24 October, a detachment of Junkers (reactionary soldiers) turned up to close down the Bolshevik printing presses; they smashed the equipment and sealed the building. It seemed that the government had scored its first victory in spite of its weak position. A male and a female worker ran to Smolny, the Soviet's headquarters. If the Military Revolutionary Committee would give them the order, the workers would bring out the Bolshevik paper. The order was given, loyal regiments were sent for and the workers opened the building and set to work; "the newspaper suppressed by the government came out under protection of the troops of a committee which was itself liable to arrest. That was insurrection. That is how it developed". Twelve hours later, soldiers would turn up at a printing plant to suppress the Petrograd Soviet paper, *Worker and Soldier*. This time there was no need to ask. The printing workers, with the help of two sailors, simply seized the car filled with printing paper, dispersed the aggressors and brought out the paper.[110] Rather than intimidating the masses, the attempts to close the press of the working class and soldiers spurred on workers' organisation and confidence, as well as strengthening the sense of a common cause between the soldiers and the workers.

The days that shook the world

When the government tried to send the Petrograd garrison which had defended the revolution in Petrograd to the front, when they moved to close the Bolshevik printing presses and began to draw up the bridges, they opened the floodgates to the insurrection. The preparation, the feverish debates and discussions in the streets, factories and barracks, had prepared vast masses of the oppressed to defend the Soviet. Wide layers of those masses also understood that the defeat of the Bolsheviks would mean the victory of the counter-revolution and the end of their hopes.

That is why the 24th and 25th look like not much more than a military exercise when taken out of the context of the previous weeks.

There was no more need of mass mobilisations. The only questions remaining were who would prevail, would the *actions* of the Bolsheviks to repulse the attacks from the government galvanise the promised defence? And they did. Trotsky paints a vivid picture of the city of Petrograd on the evening of 25 October 1917, the day that would shake the international bourgeois world to its foundations:

> In the Vyborg district opposite the headquarters of the Red Guard a whole camp was created: the street was jammed full of wagons, passenger cars and trucks. The institutions of the district were swarming with armed workers. The soviet, the duma, the trade unions, the factory and shop committees – everything in this district – were serving the cause of the insurrection. In the factories and barracks and various institutions the same thing was happening in a smaller way as throughout the whole capital: they were crowding out some and electing others, breaking the last threads of the old and strengthening the new ... At continuous meetings fresh information was given out, fighting confidence kept up and ties reinforced. The human masses were crystallising along new axes; a revolution was achieving itself.[111]

In spite of this mass mobilisation, the general opinion of the Bolsheviks' opponents was that they would be easily overthrown. John Reed comments: "That the Bolsheviki would remain in power longer than three days never occurred to anybody – except perhaps to Lenin, Trotsky, the Petrograd workers and the simple soldiers".

There are always those who, like a writer in a conservative daily at the time, sneer at Lenin's idea that every cook can govern:

> Let us suppose for a moment that the Bolsheviks do gain the upper hand. Who will govern us then: the cooks perhaps, those connoisseurs of cutlets and beefsteaks? Or maybe the firemen? The stableboys, the chauffeurs? Or perhaps the nursemaids will rush off to meetings of the Council of State between the diaper washing sessions? Who then? Where are the statesmen? Perhaps the mechanics will run the theatres, the plumbers foreign affairs, the carpenters, the post office. Who will it be? History alone will give a definitive answer to this mad ambition of the Bolsheviks.[112]

This disbelief in the ability of the masses to shape history casts its shadow over virtually all interpretations of the events of October. The lie that October was a coup, that the Bolsheviks opportunistically manipulated events to their purposes – all of these untruths are used to discredit not just the Bolsheviks, not just the revolution of 1917, but the very *idea* of workers' revolution. These are the real agendas behind historians' inability – or refusal – to acknowledge that October was a popular revolution with the backing of vast masses of working people. You only have to read the statements of those involved in the events at the time to see this reality. Their accounts highlight that shadow of elitist prejudice that blinds historians to the truth of October 1917. This truth was summed up by Martov, Lenin's long time political opponent, in a private communication in which he had no reason to tell anything but the truth:

> Understand, please, that before us after all is a victorious uprising of the proletariat – almost the entire proletariat supports Lenin and expects its social liberation from the uprising.[113]

Chapter six
The Bolsheviks and the masses

> Because of a profound misunderstanding I joined the SR party which has now passed to the side of the bourgeoisie and lent a hand to our exploiters. So that I shall not be nailed to this mast of shame, I am quitting the ranks of the chauvinists. As a conscious proletarian, I am joining the Bolshevik comrades who alone are the genuine defenders of the oppressed people.
>
> – A letter from a worker from the Aivaz works in the newspaper *Rabochii* (*The Worker*)[114]

BOTH RIGHT-WING OPPONENTS OF THE REVOLUTION and many of those who support it emphasise the role of the Bolsheviks in the victory of October. While the Bolsheviks were important, they were not all-knowing or all-powerful, simply guiding the masses along a straight line to soviet power as the standard Stalinist histories would lead us to believe. Neither did they manipulate the masses into passively accepting their rule as their detractors imagine.

In September Lenin wrote an impassioned article arguing that workers could run the state if they took power. This short article graphically highlights how deeply Lenin identified with the masses, and how the smallest aspects of their lives could take on significance in his eyes. And it shows as clearly as any weighing up of the facts of October, that Lenin was not interested in coups, but in the culmination of what he had consecrated his life to – the fight for workers' power. He tells a story about when he was hiding in some workers' home:

> The hostess puts bread on the table. The host says: "Look what fine bread. 'They' dare not give us bad bread now. And we had almost given up thinking that we'd ever get good bread in Petrograd again."

I was amazed at this class appraisal of the July Days. My thoughts had been revolving around the political significance of those events, weighing the role they played in the general course of events...and how we ought to change our slogans and alter our Party apparatus to adapt to the changed situation. As for bread, I, who had not known want, did not give it a thought. I took the bread for granted, as a by-product of the writer's work, as it were. The mind approaches the foundation of everything, the class struggle for bread, through political analysis that follows an extremely complicated and devious path.

This member of the oppressed class, however, even though one of the well-paid and quite intelligent workers, takes the bull by the horns with that astonishing simplicity and straightforwardness, with that firm determination and amazing clarity of outlook from which we intellectuals are as remote as the stars in the sky. The whole world is divided into two camps: "us", the working people, and "them", the exploiters. Not a shadow of embarrassment over what had taken place; it was just one of the battles in the long struggle between labour and capital...

"We squeezed 'them' a bit;' 'they' won't dare to lord it over us as they did before. We'll squeeze again – and chuck them out altogether", that's how the worker thinks and feels.[115]

It is not surprising that many historians present the October insurrection as just a Bolshevik coup. They want to discredit the idea of workers' revolution itself. Some are simply opposed to the mass of workers ruling. But others cannot envisage workers being able to consciously take political action. They assume that there must have been intellectuals manipulating them. It is from this elitist idea that many of the caricatures of Lenin as the power-hungry manipulator, using the workers for his own ends, are manufactured. As one social historian concluded: "[R]elated to the view of the 'dark masses' is the notion that the Bolsheviks won their following by 'manipulating' the base instincts of the masses by a fearsome combination of demagogy and lies".[116]

The months between February and October 1917 reveal in all its complexity how masses of the exploited and oppressed can come to class consciousness, how they can throw off the yoke of oppression and fight for their own rights. Some of the most interesting historical writing about the year is by social historians who used the methods of "history from below" to try to understand the events. Some of them wanted to understand how Lenin could have got such power, but their researches led them to understand that Lenin won the support of the mass of workers and peasants because his aim of workers' power became the only viable option other than military dictatorship and the destruction of all that the workers had already won. And Lenin and the Bolsheviks were the only ones clearly arguing for workers to take power.

As Lenin always argued, masses of people learn through a combination of their own experience and the arguments revolutionaries make. If a boss treats you badly, you can conclude that you should pull in your head and look after yourself, perhaps scab on your workmates and be a suck for the boss. This is a likely conclusion if there is no union, and right-wing workers or the bosses' supervisors make all the political arguments in the workplace. But if there is an alternative voice, arguing that together, workers could stand up to the boss and defend their rights, completely different ideas may take hold.

In Russia in 1917, the arguments of the Bolsheviks at times could seem marginal, outrageous, unthinkable. But increasingly they connected with workers' actual experience of the advance of the counter-revolution. As Diane Koenker, who studied the Moscow working class of 1917, explains:

> Moscow's workers had indeed become radicalized, but the process was incremental, and took place in response to *specific* economic and political factors. Textile workers, for example, did not become radicalized so much because they were dazzled by Bolshevik pie-in-the-sky promises, as some historians would like to think, but because of specific incidents. For example, when a factory manager would announce the shutdown of a plant because there was no fuel left to fire the boilers, a workers' delegation would then investigate all the firm's warehouses and discover ample

reserves. The Bolsheviks, almost alone of all the socialist parties, claimed the bourgeoisie could not be trusted, and here was proof. When incidents like these were reported in the press, or discussed in the neighbourhood tavern, the process of radicalization by experience spread.[117]

Trotsky explains how the development of class consciousness and understanding of what was needed for final victory was a very uneven process. There was not just a straight line of march with gradually developing understanding among increasing numbers of people. The attacks from the ruling class could at times propel the masses forward; at other times they pulled them backwards. The July days and their aftermath were a turning point in the process. A Moscow worker Bolshevik, Ratekhin, gives a flavour of some of the first experiences:

> I will never forget one mortally hard moment. A plenary session was assembling [of his district's soviet]... I saw there were none too many of our comrade Bolsheviks... Steklov, one of the energetic comrades, came right up close to me and, barely enunciating the words, asked: "Is it true they are working on German money...?" My heart sank with pain when I heard those questions.[118]

Even among the most advanced workers, the slanders and the offensive of the counter-revolution sapped workers' confidence. V Yakovleva, a member of the Bolshevik Central Committee and leader of wide-ranging work in Moscow, summarised the effects:

> [A]ll the reports from the localities described with one voice not only a sharp decline in the mood of the masses, but even a definite hostility to our party. In a good number of cases our speakers were beaten up. The membership fell off rapidly, and several organisations, especially in the northern provinces, even ceased to exist entirely.

Talk of expelling the Bolsheviks from the soviets forced them in some parts of Moscow to leave not only the soviets, but also the trade unions. But paradoxically, in some areas where workers were just getting involved, for example women textile workers, they moved directly to joining the Bolsheviks and were almost untouched by the reaction. Trotsky says "the July reaction established a kind of decisive watershed between the February and October Revolutions". And he explains:

> [T]he political development of the masses proceeds not in a direct line, but in a complicated curve... Objective conditions were powerfully impelling the workers, soldiers and peasants toward the banners of the Bolsheviks, but the masses were entering upon this path in a state of struggle with their own past, with their yesterday's beliefs, and partly also with their beliefs of today. At a difficult turn, at a moment of failure and disappointment, the old prejudices not yet burnt out would flare up, and the enemy would naturally seize upon these as upon an anchor of salvation... Everything about the Bolsheviks which was unclear, unusual, puzzling – the novelty of their thoughts, their audacity, their contempt for all old and new authorities – all this now suddenly acquired one simple explanation, convincing in its absurdity: They are German spies! In advancing this accusation against the Bolsheviks, the enemy were really staking their game upon the enslaved past of the people, upon the relics among them of darkness, barbarism, superstition.

But while the spread of the lie was wide, it never was deep-seated. And experience of the reaction in some places quickly educated workers to see that the attacks on the Bolsheviks were the preparation for an attack on the workers' revolution itself. Even soldiers – peasants in uniform and generally more backward than the workers – began to draw their own conclusions. By 20 July Bolshevik propaganda work had revived, and Trotsky, on his arrest on the 23rd, reported to the other prison inmates that the party's assessment was that the repression was increasing their popularity and "in the workers' districts no loss of spirit is to be observed". A meeting of workers from 27 plants in the Peterhoff district soon after passed a resolution of protest against the counter-revolutionary policy of the government. Trotsky says that by the end of July "the position of the Bolsheviks in the Petrograd factories was already restored. The workers were united under the same banners, but they were now different workers, more mature – that is, more cautious but at the same time more resolute".[119]

In the weeks from late July until the Kornilov conspiracy, delegates of workers visited the soldiers, and soldiers were brought from the front to address workers. Their stories of suffering and oppression, and of the attempts of employers and officers to turn back the gains of the revolution reinforced each other, laying the basis for a decisive rebuff of Kornilov and for a deepening understanding of the tasks ahead. It was in this period that the Committee for the Defence of Industry, which set as its goal the disorganisation and sabotage of industry, was formed. This propelled newly radicalising workers, who had not learnt the caution of the more experienced, into action. Some of the "most backward and submissive strata", as Trotsky described them, began to rise: textile workers, rubber, leather and paper workers. In Kiev, there was a "riotous strike of the night watchmen and janitors" who removed keys from elevators and put out street lights. And actions like these spread like wildfire. Trotsky says of the days of Kornilov: "The nearer you came to the district, to the factory, to the barrack, the more complete and indubitable was the leadership of the Bolsheviks".[120]

Mass support for the Bolsheviks and their demand "all power to the soviets" grew after the Kornilov coup, even though their leaders were either in jail or hiding because of the government witch hunt against them. Once Kornilov was defeated, the Bolsheviks' influence was rapidly reflected in the composition of the soviets. They won a majority in the Petrograd Soviet on 31 August, and Trotsky, who had recently joined their ranks, was elected its president. The Moscow Soviet followed five days later, with a vote of no confidence in the provisional government passed by 335 votes to 254 in this, the second most powerful soviet in the land. Kiev, the capital of Ukraine, followed a few days later, then Kazan, Baku, Nikolaev and a number of other industrial towns, along with Finnish soviets where their majorities were even stronger. Bolshevik majorities were elected in Siberia, the Urals main centre and in the Volga towns of the Donetz Basin. In some regions reports came in that the Soviet had taken power into its hands.

This radical shift to support for the Bolsheviks was highlighted by the Moscow garrison. In June 70 percent supported the peasant party, the Socialist Revolutionaries, and by September 90 percent supported the Bolsheviks. On 30 August, the Petrograd garrison, numbering about 60,000 passed this resolution: "The Petrograd garrison no longer recognises the provisional government. The Petrograd Soviet is our government. We will obey only the orders of the Petrograd Soviet, through the Military Revolutionary Committee".[121]

While the SRs maintained the majority support of the peasantry, by September over half the SR representatives had split with the main party over the issue of power. These Left SRs went on to join the Soviet government. In the Second All-Russian Congress of Soviets beginning on the night of the insurrection in October there was a large Bolshevik majority. The Congress opened with 650 delegates; 390 were Bolshevik delegates, even though many of them weren't actually members of the party. Overwhelming support for the insurrection itself, even among non-Bolsheviks, was evident. Out of the 670 delegates asked their view on power, 505 responded that they were for all power to the soviets. As Trotsky remarks, the Mensheviks and Socialist Revolutionaries had completely squandered their political capital from the February Revolution. In the June Congress the Compromisers had 600 of 882 delegates. Now they had less than a quarter of the votes, and an overwhelming majority of these were "Lefts" who veered towards the Bolsheviks. The delegates counted 900 before the end, but the proportion of Bolsheviks held steady.

Morgan Philips Price, who was originally opposed to the Bolsheviks, argues that:

> The government of M Kerensky fell before the Bolshevik insurgents because it had no supporters in the country. The bourgeois parties and the generals of the Staff disliked it because it would not establish a military dictatorship. The revolutionary democracy lost faith in it because after eight months it had neither given land to the peasants nor established state control of industries nor advanced the cause of the Russian peace programme...[122]

The role of the Bolsheviks

By August it was not just the workers who were more mature. The Bolshevik members had been tested. Those who wavered in July showed they were not reliable when the most extreme tests were faced, those who did not flinch were hardened by the experience, their confidence and their authority among those who looked to them confirmed. It would be only a matter of weeks before Lenin began agitating for the Bolsheviks to grasp the nettle and organise the final insurrection to transfer power to the soviets. Sukhanov, who belonged to the Menshevik Party that shattered in the course of the revolution, was no admirer of Lenin and the Bolsheviks. But he drew a graphic picture of their role and their relationship to the masses:

> [T]he Bolsheviks worked zealously and unceasingly. They were among the masses, in the factories, every day and all the time... They became the party of the masses because they were always there, guiding both in great things and small the whole life of the factories and barracks. The masses lived and breathed together with the Bolsheviks. They were wholly in the hands of the party of Lenin and Trotsky.[123]

But this does not completely explain the politics which made their unceasing activity effective. We can assume many Mensheviks were just as devoted to their political activity; but their wavering, compromising politics played into the hands of the reaction. Ultimately, those Mensheviks who sincerely wanted the revolution to continue joined the Bolsheviks, those who remained in their party ended up supporting the counter-revolution. The Bolsheviks' ability to win the leadership of the revolutionary masses flowed from their whole political program and political approach. Trotsky argues:

> The wholeness of the Bolshevik policy was due to the fact that, in contrast to the "democratic parties", the Bolsheviks were free from unexpressed or semi-expressed gospels reducing themselves in the last analysis to a defence of private property ... on the left too there were the anarchists, the Maximalists, the Left Social Revolutionaries, trying to crowd them out. But these groups too – none of them ever emerged from its impotent state.

> What distinguished Bolshevism was that it subordinated the subjective goal, the defence of the interests of the popular masses, to the laws of revolution as an objectively conditioned process. The scientific discovery of these laws, and first of all those which govern the movement of popular masses, constituted the basis of the Bolshevik strategy.[124]

Remember Lenin's words to the military conference in June: events should not be anticipated, time is on our side. He banked everything on his understanding of the logic of events unfolding around them. He had argued in July: "the masses are still looking for the 'easiest' way out – through the bloc of the Cadets with the bloc of the Socialist Revolutionaries and the Mensheviks... But there is no way out".[125]

He did not predict events in some mystical way, or just indulge in wishful thinking. His whole approach was based on his general analysis that world capitalism was in a deathly crisis, and this set both limits and possibilities for what could eventuate. In an article in July analysing the situation, he wrote:

> The Socialist-Revolutionary and Menshevik parties could have given Russia many a reform by agreement with the bourgeoisie. But the objective situation in world politics is revolutionary and it cannot be dealt with by reforms.
>
> The imperialist war is crushing the peoples and threatens to crush them completely. The petty-bourgeois democrats can perhaps stave off disaster for a while. But it is only the revolutionary proletariat that can prevent a tragic end.[126]

But it was not just analysis of the political situation that gave the Bolsheviks their ability to relate to the masses. Trotsky again:

> The toilers are guided in their struggle not only by their demands, not only their needs, but by their life experiences. Bolshevism had absolutely no taint of any aristocratic scorn for the independent experience of the masses. On the contrary, the Bolsheviks took this for their point of departure and built upon it. That was one of their great points of superiority.[127]

Trotsky points out that the Mensheviks and Socialist Revolutionaries tried to talk their way out of difficulties and find compromises, the Bolsheviks confronted the difficulties. And the Bolsheviks' activity, their tactics and strategies were always based on "an analysis of the objective situation, a testing of slogans upon facts, a serious attitude to the enemy". This was what gave a "special strength and power of conviction to the Bolshevik agitation". The Bolsheviks did not exaggerate success, or try to win by mere shouting, they did not bend the truth of events to satisfy their own arguments. "The school of Lenin was a school of revolutionary realism", so much so that Trotsky says the facts supplied by Bolshevik publications at the time are some of the most reliable sources.

> "We are not charlatans", said Lenin immediately after his arrival. "We must base ourselves only upon the consciousness of the masses. Even if it is necessary to remain in a minority... We must not be afraid to be a minority... We will carry on the work of criticism in order to free the masses from deceit... Our line will prove right. All the oppressed will come to us... They have no other way out." Here we have the Bolshevik policy, comprehensible from beginning to end as the direct opposite of demagoguism and adventurism.[128]

One worker expressed the same point in his own words: "the Bolsheviks have always said: 'It is not we who will persuade you, but life itself.' And now [in September] the Bolsheviks have triumphed because life has proved their tactics right".[129]

Sukhanov, the intellectual par excellence, moderate, "cultured", member of the compromising bloc, dismissed the radicalisation of the masses: "Their Bolshevism was nothing but hatred for the coalition and longing for land and peace". It was hardly a minor matter that these masses of peasants in uniform and workers in the factories had come to understand that to get the land their oppressors had to be overthrown, that to get peace the soviets had to take power, and what's more, that only the Bolsheviks of all the parties on offer were prepared to carry the revolution through in order to get land, bread and peace. That "nothing but" reveals the elitism, the "taint of aristocratic scorn" that cuts off virtually all of the Bolsheviks' critics from understanding the masses. As Trotsky says in his *History*:

> The insignificance of the democrats, even the most leftward, resulted from this very distrust – the distrust of "educated" sceptics – in those dark masses who grasp a phenomenon wholesale, not bothering about details and nuances. This intellectual, pseudo-aristocratic, squeamish attitude toward the people was foreign to Bolshevism, hostile to its very nature. The Bolsheviks were not lily-handed, literary friends of the masses, not pedants. They were not afraid of those backward strata now for the first time lifting themselves out of the dregs. The Bolsheviks took the people as preceding history had created them, and as they were called to achieve the revolution. The Bolsheviks saw it as their mission to stand at the head of the people.[130]

Chapter seven
After October

THE SECOND ALL-RUSSIAN CONGRESS OF SOVIETS opened at 11.45pm on 26 October. And at the same time a telegram from Lenin was flying through the airwaves to every corner of Russia:

> To the citizens of Russia
>
> The provisional government has been overthrown. State power has passed into the hands of the organ of the Petrograd Soviet of Workers' and Soldiers' Deputies, the Military Revolutionary Committee, which stands at the head of the Petrograd proletariat and garrison.
>
> The cause for which the people have struggled – the immediate proposal of a democratic peace, the elimination of landlord estates, workers' control over production, the creation of a soviet government – the triumph of this cause has been assured.
>
> Long live the workers', soldiers', and peasants' revolution!
>
> The Military Revolutionary Committee of the Petrograd Soviet of Workers' and Soldiers' Deputies.[131]

In the Congress itself, these aims were confirmed: immediate negotiations for a just peace, confiscation of the great landed estates to be given to the peasant committees for redistribution, workers' control over industry. This Congress was not just notable for its proclamations. The composition was strikingly different from the last one in June, as was the political line-up. Of course these three aspects were all entwined. In June intellectuals and army officers had been prominent. John Reed graphically describes a very different one now:

> [T]he new delegates come in – burly, bearded soldiers, workmen in black blouses, a few long-haired peasants. The girl in charge – a member of Plekhanov's Edinstvo group – smiled contemptuously. "These are very different people from the delegates to the first Sezd", she remarked. "See how rough and ignorant they look! The Dark People..." It was true: the depths of Russia had been stirred, and it was the bottom which came uppermost now.[132]

That Menshevik woman, by talking to the revolution's chronicler, inadvertently left a clue for history as to why the Mensheviks' representation had plummeted from over 200 delegates in June to fewer than 70; why they now confronted 390 Bolsheviks out of 650 delegates and another possible 190 pro-Bolshevik Left SRs. And history gave its answer. The October Revolution consolidated the gains since February for masses of people in Russia; but it was also a huge leap into the future.

First the decrees. They called on the belligerent countries to start immediate negotiations for a just, democratic peace. They abolished private ownership of land "for ever", decreed that "all land, whether state, crown, monastery, church, factory, entailed, private, public, peasant, etc.... will be confiscated without compensation and become the property of the whole people and pass into the use of all those who cultivate it". Lenin, with the humility typical of him and a lack of bravado, simply adopted the land program of the peasant-based SRs and wrote it up as government policy. The peasants want the land? Let them organise its redistribution as they demand. The enslaved national minorities of the Russian empire were given the right to independence up to and including secession. And workers' control over production was decreed as the basis for the reorganisation of the economy for the good of the population.

Inspiring as they were, decrees could not solve the problems the revolutionary government faced. But the workers, soldiers and peasants of Russia would, against incredible odds for three years, repulse an international counter-revolution launched against them, and they would leave a sketch of what the masses are capable of. The overturn of exploitation, placing control in the hands of the exploited, led to an explosion of experimentation. Anything seemed possible, from equal pay, to communal child care, eating and housework to free women from drudgery, to control over one's sexuality. The sense of exhilarating joy enthused poets, artists, architects and engineers to rethink how both the physical world and the imaginary could be transformed not for profits, the comforts and enjoyment of a privileged minority, or the glorification of a repressive state, but for all. Experimentation in every field burst the limits set by class society, searching for a new truth for a world worth living in. As an example of the atmosphere, just think of Trotsky – travelling from one end of Russia to the other and back again, organising the Red Army in the civil war from early in 1918, fighting back imperialist armies' invasions and the White armies of the Russian counter-revolution – writing a series of articles on literature and art![133]

The economy had to be transformed so that wealth was directed to consumption for the vast majority instead of the obscene luxury of the elite, or for the accumulation of more wealth for them. And Russia was faced with devastation caused by the war and deliberate sabotage by the owners of industry. Economic and social revolution stepped forward hand in hand. Some of the legal changes promulgated by the Soviet went far beyond simply economic reorganisation. They opened the possibility of individual freedoms and personal liberation. The Bolsheviks had the oppressed in mind as they legislated these changes. Trotsky said:

> The Revolution is before and above all the awakening of humanity ... A revolution does not deserve its name if, with all its might and all the means at its disposal, it does not help the woman – twofold and threefold enslaved as she has been in the past – to get on the road of individual and social progress.[134]

In the first year, the decrees of the Soviet government included universal suffrage, ended the authority of heads of families, abolished the right of inheritance, established divorce and civil laws that made marriage a voluntary relationship free of state and church control. Illegitimacy was abolished as a legal concept, paid maternity leave before and after birth was enshrined in law, adultery, incest and homosexuality were removed from the criminal code. Lenin had argued both against ideas about the need to limit the birth rate and for abortion rights and access to all known means of contraception in a debate in *Pravda*, the Bolshevik paper, in 1913.[135] But it was not until 1920 that a majority was won to provide abortion on demand. Nevertheless, it was the first such reform in the world, and in advance of most countries to this day. All of these gains, backed up by the eight-hour day, equal pay, literacy programs, child care and communal kitchens, provided the basis for women to take control over their own bodies, for their economic and sexual freedom, and to take their place in public life.

Some historians suggest that the Bolsheviks did not purposely decriminalise homosexuality, they simply refused to recognise its existence and so it disappeared in the revolutionary decrees. However, revolutionary socialists had for decades led the way in defending sexual freedom between consenting individuals. Like all revolutionaries at the time, the Bolsheviks thought the family as an institution governing sexuality and personal life would eventually die away once class society was ended. It was logical for them to deliberately remove state repression of sexuality from the law. As one historian of sexuality in Russia points out, the Bolsheviks were associated with the stand taken by the German Social Democratic Party: "The link was clearest in the Russians' enthusiastic embrace of August Bebel's theories on sexual politics in his extremely popular *Women and Socialism* (1879)".

Bebel was the first member of parliament anywhere in the world to speak in support of legislation legalising same-sex acts. And he amended his book to include an argument that same-sex love is as natural as any other. The Bolsheviks, like all other Marxists, understood that sexual oppression is the result of class society, and therefore sexual liberation was as integral to a workers' revolution as the economic and social changes that the revolution made possible.

Thus it is not surprising that this study found that "[p]opular expressions of homosexual emancipation from post-1917 Soviet sources...suggest that self-identified homosexuals in Russia believed the revolution had ended the state's 'refusal of the private'...licensing their right to love".[136]

However, legislating for the possibility of freedom, taking over industry and defeating the old state did not make liberation inevitable. To make the promise a reality, resources had to be found. But from the start, feeding the cities was the first priority. Hunger had partly driven the radicalisation of 1917, it could not be wished away. Industry was operating at production levels below those that existed before the war, and capitalists who had been sabotaging the economy all year now stepped up their efforts as workers struggled to take control. And in the ensuing civil war, which did not end until early 1921, industrial production dropped to one fifth of its pre-1914 levels. The working class who had carried through the revolution, had given it its power, was devastated. Almost all of the most class conscious had gone to fight, and the cities shrank. By 1920 Petrograd was a mere 40 percent of its size at the time of the revolution.

And yet in the midst of this suffering, the cultural, creative and spiritual energy of the masses was astonishing. One hundred and twenty-five thousand literacy schools were set up, factories established education commissions that put on theatre productions, poetry readings and orchestral concerts that were patronised by huge numbers of working women and men. The schools could not start on time in 1918 because the teachers were debating the latest and best methods of instruction.

However, socialism cannot be built by sheer willpower and determination. And so now we must face the tragedy of the overthrow of this first and only workers' state in history that inspired workers around the globe at the time, that still inspires anyone who hates capitalism and agrees it should and can be replaced by a society of which we had but a glimpse after 1917.

Chapter eight

The first step in the international socialist revolution

TROTSKY, ADDRESSING THE DELEGATES of the Second All-Russian Congress of Soviets on 25 October, emphasised that their seizure of power had the potential to spark international revolution; indeed their future depended on it:

> We rest all our hopes on the possibility that our revolution will unleash the European revolution. If the revolting peoples of Europe do not crush imperialism, then we will be crushed – that is indubitable. Either the Russian revolution will raise the whirlwind of struggle in the west, or the capitalists of all countries will crush our revolution.[137]

This was not just some quibble or rhetoric. Lenin repeated the point in January 1918: "The absolute truth is that without a revolution in Germany we shall perish". Trotsky reiterates, writing over ten years later:

> [I]t could not have entered the mind of any Bolshevik at that time to protest against placing the fate of the Soviet Republic in an official speech in the name of the Bolshevik Party, in direct dependence upon the development of the international revolution.

He thought it necessary to emphasise this point because this tradition, this foundation stone of Bolshevik theory and practice, had in the meantime been overthrown by Stalin. In 1924 Stalin had proclaimed that the aim of the Bolshevik Party was "socialism in one country". From then on, Stalin and his henchmen conducted a vitriolic campaign against the idea that the fate of the revolution depended on the success or failure of revolutions in the West.

They condemned it as "Trotskyism" and alien to the true traditions of Lenin and the Bolsheviks.

Of course, whether this argument is part of the Bolshevik tradition or not does not prove whether it is correct or false. It does however illustrate the profound departure from Bolshevik traditions that Stalin's regime, which claimed to be building "socialism in one country", represented.

But here we want to understand the defeat of the revolution, how Stalin could come to power. A few points can clarify why the emphasis on the necessity of international revolution is important in Marxist theory. Socialism is not a utopia that can be conjured up by sheer will power. Like all other societies, it requires the material basis that makes its existence possible. Socialism is a classless society based not on the subsistence of pre-class societies such as Australian Indigenous societies, but on the basis of the technologies and level of productive power class societies have developed. Socialism was impossible in the Middle Ages, or in the time of the slave societies of ancient Greece and Rome. Once society was riven by class divisions, in which a tiny minority live off a surplus of wealth and goods produced by the labour of the vast majority, then the only material basis for a new classless society was abundance. Only with abundance could the surplus be used to raise the living standards of all and not just a minority.

Capitalism, a system of rapacious competition, has created the material basis for socialism. It has also created a special kind of exploited class, one that is organised into collective, co-operative work, and which has to organise collectively in order to advance its interests. This class is the proletariat or working class. Marx and Engels called them "the grave-diggers of capitalism". So by the beginning of the twentieth century, the material basis for socialism existed on a world scale. But it did not make socialism inevitable. The working class has to overthrow the system, and this means conscious class struggle.

The existence of this material basis for socialism on a world scale did not in 1917, and still does not today, mean that individual countries can build socialism while the rest of the globe is dominated by capitalist competition. Capitalism, because it is an international system, has created an international division of labour. So no one country is self-sufficient. Trade is imperative because of the interdependence of economies for basic necessities and the materials needed for industry. This interlocking of economies means a workers' state, unless joined by others that are reorganising production on a collective basis to provide for human need, rather than driven by the ethos of competition, will inevitably be drawn back into the competitive drive imposed by capitalist production.

Tony Cliff, in a path-breaking book in the late 1940s, *State Capitalism in Russia*, built on the materialist analysis of the bureaucracy that Trotsky had begun in *The Revolution Betrayed*. They both argued that the increasingly undemocratic, authoritarian practices of the state bureaucracy were the result of its isolation and pressure from the world capitalist system.[138]

Cliff, unlike Trotsky, concluded that Stalin's bureaucracy had presided over a complete counter-revolution in the period of the first five-year plan of 1928–1933. His detailed economic analysis showed clearly the change in orientation that marked the death of the last vestiges of workers' power and the triumph of a new ruling class with the same emphasis on competition and accumulation of capital at the expense of workers as that of capitalists the world over.

> Under capitalism the consumption of the masses is subordinated to accumulation. [The ratio can vary, but] the basic relationship remains. If we follow the history of Russia from October, we find that until the advent of the Five-Year Plan this subordination did not exist, but from then on expresses itself in unprecedented brutality.[139]

Gross output as percentage of consumption vs. production

	1913	1928	1932	1937	1940	1942
Production	44.3	32.8	53.3	57.8	61.0	62.2
Consumption	55.7	67.2	46.7	42.2	39.0	37.8

He documents the loss of any vestiges of workers' influence on the bureaucracy, the catastrophic falls in workers' industrial activity, the atomisation of workers by introducing incentive schemes such as piece work and bonuses and increases in the rate of exploitation by sheer speed-ups. Stalin himself summed up what was driving all these changes:

> To slacken the pace of industrialisation would mean to lag behind; and those who lag behind are beaten ... We are fifty or one hundred years behind the advanced countries. We must make good this lag in ten years. Either we do it or they crush us.[140]

In other words, they had succumbed to the competitive drive of capitalism. Other historians identify the same turning point, and highlight the dynamic of military competition which replaced any residual ideas of cooperative planning to build a society based on human need. Michael Reiman, historian of the birth of Stalin's' regime, argues that in about 1927:

> With increasing urgency, demands were made for the quickest possible strengthening of the army and the defensive capacity of the Soviet state in general, for a reorientation of the economy and social relations towards a perspective of imminent war, and for more extensive industrialisation.[141]

This statement from the Congress of the ruling CPSU in December 1927 reinforces the point:

> Bearing in mind the possibility of a military attack ... it is essential in elaborating the five-year plan to devote maximum attention to a most rapid development of those branches of the economy in general and industry in particular on which the main role will fall in securing the defence and economic stability of the country in war time.[142]

Again, it is the coercive competitive pressure to accumulate – the central dynamic of capitalism – that was reflected in Stalin's proclamation and openly stated by the ruling body.

Many books have been written about the degeneration of the Bolshevik Party and the rise of Stalin's authoritarian state. However, this emphasis on the detail of that transformation, limited to the events inside Russia, does not *explain* why it happened. It does nothing more than *describe* the effects of the isolation of the revolution. Once the USSR is understood in relation to the world economy, we can see the pressure that undermined the commitment to workers' power.

By the end of 1917 the economy was already in severe crisis from a combination of the war and deliberate sabotage by the capitalists. Lenin assessed the situation just before the October insurrection: "[T]he complete disruption of Russia's economic life has now reached a point where catastrophe is unavoidable".[143] These economic conditions set limits that could not be overcome by will power or good intentions. As Marx said, humans make their own history, but they do so in given conditions not of their own making. A materialist understanding of how objective circumstances place limits on what is possible is essential if we are to arrive at an accurate assessment of the years after 1917. There are those such as anarchists who give lip service to the idea of workers' control, but who refuse to face reality, charging the Bolsheviks with responsibility for the decline in mass participation in the workers' factory committee and soviets. They accuse the Bolsheviks of deliberate authoritarian practices and the imposition of unnecessary "law and order" as early as 1918. They argue that these developments were the outcome of Bolshevik principles, thereby beginning an inevitable journey down the road to Stalin's dictatorial rule.[144] Similar arguments are made by Diane Koenker, a social historian who provided sensitive insights into the developments of 1917 towards the mass popular support for the Bolsheviks:

> [T]he stamp of the current Soviet regime was not made in October 1917... [T]he features of one-party rule, of terror, and Stalinist compulsion that influence our perceptions of the Soviet Union today, were not necessarily inherent in the process by which the Bolsheviks *came* to power. Rather, we must look to the critical period after October, at what the Bolsheviks did to hold power...[145]

But none of these arguments are grounded in any attempt to understand the material conditions and the problems the workers' state confronted. They assume that history is driven by the ideas in people's heads. If you want socialism, then you can build it no matter what the circumstances, which amounts to another version of Stalin's "socialism in one country". In the conditions workers had to combat, disorder was tantamount to sabotage of the workers' state. Any government trying to represent the interests of the workers' state in the hope of getting help from a new workers' state had the right – even the duty – to discipline those who undermined production.

Reports were coming in from everywhere of famine and epidemics and the threat of counter-revolution as people lashed out, crying out for help. Speaking at a meeting in May 1918, Trotsky read from telegrams he had: "Viksi, Nizhni-Novgorod province: the shops are empty, work is going badly, shortage of 30 percent of the workers through starvation. Men collapsing with hunger at their benches". From Bryansk: "Terrible mortality, especially of children, around the factories of Maltsov and Bryansk typhus is raging". There were no raw materials or fuel for industry, the oil fields of Baku and other regions and the coal mines ground to a standstill. Workers forced to scavenge for a living, or desperately trying to keep loved ones alive in the chaos found it increasingly difficult to participate in the political life of the committees. Lenin himself warned of the dangers the party faced. He was not interested in pretending they were marching on unhindered to socialism. His whole political practice was premised on facing reality first and foremost: "It must be recognised that the party's proletarian policy is determined at present not by its rank and file, but by the immense and undivided authority of the tiny sections that might be called the party's 'old guard'".[146]

But without material help from a wealthy country, the problems could not be overcome. To try to hold on while they fomented revolutions in Europe, the Bolsheviks used the mechanisms of the state, even bringing in specialists from the old regime to organise departments and industry. This was clearly not socialism, but as Lenin called it, a form of state capitalism. It was not their goal, but it was necessary and defensible as a temporary state of affairs and while their international policies were aimed at international revolution. Again, Lenin did not flinch from the reality as things continued to worsen towards the end of his life:

> Let us look at Moscow. Who is leading whom? The 4,700 responsible communists [leading] the mass of bureaucrats, or the other way round? I do not seriously think you can say the communists are leading this mass. To be honest they are not the leaders but the led.

So the revolution was in danger from very early on. This is not the same as saying that there is a continuous line from Lenin to Stalin. Lenin did not have confidence in Stalin; he moved to have him removed from his role in the leadership of the party before he (Lenin) died in January 1924. For the Stalinist state to be established, a complete counter-revolution had to be carried out, even after several years of these terrible and debilitating conditions.[147]

The declaration in 1924 that their aim was "socialism in one country" is the ideological justification for Stalin's terror and bureaucracy, not a call to hold on while the international revolution unfolds. Apologists for the Stalinist regime say: What else could they do? The workers' state had to survive in a hostile world. But this is precisely the point. To survive in that hostile world is to capitulate to its rules and economic dynamic.

The only alternative was to continue to foster the revolution in other countries and to maintain as many of the advances of the workers' state as possible. That is why the Bolsheviks put a great effort into forming a new, Communist Third International (the Comintern) to replace the discredited Second International that had fractured when its affiliates almost universally supported the imperialist World War I. The Bolsheviks intervened in the struggles that swept Europe after 1917 to try to educate revolutionaries in the politics, strategies and tactics that could bring victory to their movements.[148]

The Kronstadt rebellion

In the circumstances of Russia, given the backward nature of the economy, plus the destruction wrought by the world war and then three years of civil war, foreign invasion and economic blockade by the West, the options narrowed very quickly. In 1921 this confronts us in all its stark reality. A sign that the workers' state was in dire trouble was the Kronstadt rebellion in March. This former centre of revolutionary zeal, previously a strong base for the Bolsheviks (now renamed as the Communist Party of the Soviet Union) became a flashpoint for all the discontents bred by three years of bitter civil war and the resulting poverty and devastation.

Now that the threat of the Whites (counter-revolutionary forces) had receded, the suffering was increasingly laid at the door of the Communist Party. The Bolsheviks' brutal crushing of the Kronstadt revolt is often held up as evidence that it was the very nature of the party that led to the Stalinist bureaucracy of later years. A more accurate assessment is what Lenin said at the time: "The Kronstadt events were like a flash of lightning which threw more of a glare upon reality than anything else".[149]

It may be legitimate to argue that the Bolsheviks over-reacted, although it cannot be discounted that a victory for the rebellion would have opened the way to a new offensive from the Whites, who were backing it. Anarchists and others who hold up this rebellion and the Bolsheviks' response argue that this shows that the Bolsheviks were authoritarian from the start. The Kronstadt rebellion is held up as a revolutionary challenge to the Bolsheviks' totalitarian dictatorship. However the most recent archives available reveal a completely different picture. Kronstadt was no longer a stronghold of revolutionary soldiers. But the revolutionary soldiers still there actually organised *against* the rebellion, as did workers on the Island. The uprising was led by pro-tsarist generals who said openly that their call for "soviets without Bolsheviks" was just a way of cloaking their action in the rhetoric of the revolution, that they intended taking power themselves.[150] No doubt they were able to tap into growing discontent among layers of the population who were not steeped in the revolutionary traditions of the most advanced workers, but that does not make it legitimate. It was a rebellion with backing from counter-revolutionaries against a workers' state under siege. In early 1921 it was still possible to hope that the revolutionary movements in some European countries might triumph. It would have been sheer capitulation and abandonment of the revolutionary goals for which millions had made such sacrifices to have risked the regime's survival because of the rising discontent.

The Kronstadt tragedy was, as Lenin realised, a blinding revelation of the drastic circumstances the revolution faced. It was not any part of the cause of its defeat. To argue that it was is to ignore the problem of isolation and therefore to accept the Stalinist ideology that socialism can be built in one country. And in light of the latest archival evidence it is tantamount to supporting the outright counter-revolution. Lenin spelt out what was necessary, if they were to go on to build socialism, at the Party Congress in March 1921:

> [H]ere industrial workers are in a minority, and the petty farmers are the vast majority. In such a country, the socialist revolution can triumph only on two conditions. First, if it is given timely support by a socialist revolution in one or several advanced countries... The second condition is agreement between the proletariat, which is exercising its dictatorship, that is, holds the state power, and the majority of the peasant population.[151]

With these two problems in mind, the Communist Party Congress, with hardly any debate or dissent, introduced what became known as the New Economic Policy (NEP) which ended grain requisitioning from the peasants. Instead they would be taxed and able to use whatever profits they could make as they decided. In other words, it allowed the reintroduction of the market. In fact, to try to hold on with the prospect of being rescued by the international revolution, the Congress conceded virtually all of the demands of the Kronstadters except their anti-democratic call for "soviets without Bolsheviks". Perhaps if the Bolsheviks had made these concessions more quickly, they could have spared the lives of those killed in the fighting that put down the rebellion. But let's be clear. If this had not led to a resurgence of the reactionaries, if it had avoided violence – none of which was inevitable – *it would not have made one iota of a difference to the outcome* of the revolution in the long run. Kronstadt, the reintroduction of the market, the bureaucratic degeneration of the party as it ruled over an increasingly impossible situation – none of these are the *cause* of the counter-revolution that engulfed them. They are the *effect* of the failure of the revolutions in the West and the isolation of the workers' state in Russia.

Trotsky's struggle against Stalin and the importance of theory

Gradually, through a series of factional struggles and attacks on anyone who opposed him, Stalin built up a bureaucratic layer around himself, and eliminated all opponents. Almost the whole of the Old Bolshevik cadre of any stature from the revolutionary years who did not die of natural causes and who stayed active was murdered by the Stalinist apparatus in one way or another. Trotsky, who had been exiled in 1929, was eventually assassinated at his home in Mexico by Stalin's agents in 1940. If the nature of the Bolshevik Party was the reason a bureaucracy emerged, why did its cadre have to be removed from the process? The fact was, Stalin had to deny, debauch and overturn every Marxist tradition of the party in order to consolidate his bureaucratic rule. He was able to do this, not because he was right, not because he was more politically astute than others, or because he was the inheritor of Lenin's authority, but because he was swimming with the historical tide.

Trotsky, his most consistent and determined rival, needed to be able to appeal to a class-conscious working class that could mobilise to defend the soviets' democracy, that could defend their conditions and limit the bureaucracy's growing power. The working class as we have seen was severely depleted and exhausted from the deprivations of the civil war, and many of the most class conscious were the ones to fight and die on the front lines. Nevertheless grassroots opposition to Stalin persisted. In 1927, a turning point in the development of the new state, Stalin's regime was under considerable pressure. The economy was sliding into crisis, and it was becoming increasingly clear that Trotsky and not Stalin was advocating the correct policy in revolutionary China. A leadership besieged and divided looks weak. And Trotsky's

United Opposition with Zinoviev and his supporters took advantage of this. Their campaigning showed that there was still working-class opposition that was a threat to Stalin's march to despotism, "spreading like a river flood" according to Michael Reiman in *The Birth of Stalinism*.

The opposition organised meetings of industrial workers in Ivanovo-Voznesensk, Leningrad (Petrograd renamed) and Moscow. At one chemical plant in Moscow there were shouts of "Down with Stalin's dictatorship!"[152] At a Party forum in July Stalin tried to go on the offensive to lay the basis to expel the opposition. But the leadership were unable to cow the opposition and came off second best, giving rise to a joke – "Stalin, not Trotsky, has had to clip his claws". Illegal and semi-legal meetings were happening around the country and opposition literature was widespread. On the day the Party Congress opened, just days before the tenth anniversary of the October Revolution, it appeared to have had some impact. The crowd of 100,000 cheered the United Opposition figures. And opposition activity was evident from Leningrad to Ukraine, Transcaucasia, Siberia, the Urals and Moscow in spite of ever increasing repression and intimidation.

However, for Trotsky and his supporters to defeat Stalin it would have taken a revolutionary upsurge by the working class and these shows of defiance were very far from that. So why couldn't they mobilise a more significant challenge from below? Tony Cliff explains:

> [M]any writers look to the psychological traits of the contenders, Stalin being more cunning and a better organiser than Trotsky. This explanation is curious. Trotsky, the organiser of the October Revolution and of the Red Army inferior to Stalin? Such an explanation, even if it describes Stalin's nasty character, gives him far too much honour as the demiurge of history.
>
> It was the objective conditions that determined how successful the Opposition could be.[153]

Others seeking an explanation for Stalin's victory over Trotsky point to the many tactical errors Trotsky made, and even major concessions in the ideological struggle. For example, hampered by an alliance with Zinoviev in the United Opposition, formed in mid-1926, he allowed

Zinoviev to produce material on the Chinese Revolution in the name of the Opposition that was at best inadequate and in part gave a downright false account of Trotsky's arguments. Trotsky admitted as much later.[154] But we need to have a sense of proportion. Such tactical blunders and compromises made it more difficult for Trotsky to build on a firm basis and provide a clear ideological refutation of Stalin, but they did not determine the course of history. We can leave the last word on this point to Cliff:

> One should be clear about the relation between Trotsky's errors and their consequences. The disproportion between the two was a result of the reactionary character of the historical stage. Not a few mistakes were committed by the Bolshevik leaders during 1917 and the period of the civil war. But the sweep of the revolution repaired the errors. Now the march of reaction exacerbated the impact of every error committed by Trotsky.
>
> Russia's economic backwardness, the weakness of the proletariat, the rise of the kulak [rich peasants], NEPman and bureaucrat, and above all the defeat of the international revolution, underlined the massive cleft between Trotsky's great aims and the puny means at his disposal.[155]

Which returns us to the key question: that of the international revolution. The most drastic consequence of the developing bureaucracy was the counter-revolutionary influence of the increasingly reactionary and bureaucratic Communist Party of the Soviet Union on the left internationally. From the fifth congress of the Comintern in 1923 the increasingly bureaucratised party still retained its influence over revolutionaries from other countries. But the Russians' advice was increasingly coloured by their desire to survive as an ever more self-aware ruling group rather than to foster revolution. As in all historical scenarios, developments do not simply proceed along a straight line with a preordained end point. Each action taken closes off options; or they lead down paths radically different from those embarked on.

The German Revolution

In November 1918 a sailors' mutiny in Kiel had sparked the German Revolution on which the Bolsheviks staked the future of the Russian Revolution. Workers' and soldiers' councils sprang up around Germany and the state virtually collapsed. A situation of dual power emerged, similar to that in Russia after February 1917. The CPSU leaders proved incapable of guiding the German Communist Party (KPD) to victory. But the situation was not finally resolved until October 1923 when the German Communist Party leaders missed one last opportunity, after five years of desperate struggles, for the working class to attempt a seizure of power. Exhausted, workers were on the retreat after that and the right was on the offensive, with the Nazis on the rise.

The failure of the KPD in October 1923 ended the prospect of revolution in Germany, a catastrophic blow to the prospects for Russia. In 1927 the devastating disaster inflicted on the Chinese Revolution and the Chinese Communist Party by the intervention of the Stalinist CPSU, over the protests of Trotsky, were becoming evident. A revolutionary situation existed. If workers had taken power as looked possible, this would have raised the possibility of reviving the genuinely revolutionary traditions of the Bolsheviks in Russia and inspiring a revival of the movements in Europe. Instead Comintern policy resulted in a reactionary nationalist government in China, which in turn resulted in the virtual destruction of the urban-based Chinese Communist Party.

So as late as 1927 we can see that if the opponents of Stalin had received stronger and clearer support from revolutionaries in the Comintern, Stalin and his surrounding bureaucrats may well have faced an entirely different future. If Trotsky had prevailed in the debates over China in the Comintern and the Chinese Communist Party had led a successful revolution, the history not just of China but also of Russia and then the whole of Europe could have been different. The opposition forces in Russia may have been able to gather wider forces if they had been able to prove their policies in practice, combined with the inspiration a victory somewhere could have injected into their movement and those around them. Instead of an authoritarian state in Russia, reaction in China and the rise of fascism in Germany and Italy, workers may have turned the tide of history back towards the promise of socialism that had been on the agenda ten years earlier. But for this to happen the Comintern would have had to have revolutionary organisations that were clear about the tasks they faced in overthrowing capitalism and with some experience of intervening in struggles.

In country after country after about 1929, rather than building genuinely revolutionary organisations, the Communist Parties were increasingly nationalist in outlook, led by time-servers and sycophants, and guided by politics that now had no relationship to the Bolshevik traditions of workers' power.[156] Anyone who raised doubts or supported Trotsky was hounded from the CPs or expelled.

The theory of socialism in one country was a reactionary, anti-Marxist utopia, the foundation stone for the ideology of a new rising bureaucracy ruling over the ashes of the revolution of 1917. That is why Trotsky included an appendix to his *History* in which he documented, chapter and verse, that putting the Russian Revolution in the context of the international struggle for socialism was an absolute and unquestioned principle among not just leading Bolsheviks, but also the rank-and-file members and even those workers, soldiers and sailors influenced by them.[157]

So could there have been an alternative? Once Stalin's clique got control and it was clear they were abandoning the revolutionary goals of the party, Trotsky and his supporters followed the only alternative open to genuine revolutionaries who still supported the Marxist idea of socialism as the self-emancipation of the working class. They began to organise opposition to these developments. They fought on every front: the question of democracy, the policies adopted by the Comintern, domestic policies that were shifting the balance from consumption to accumulation, and on questions of theory. It's tempting to see the mistakes Trotsky made both in analysis and tactics in this fight as the explanation of his defeat. But the historic tragedy was that without a successful revolution somewhere else the rise of a new ruling class was inevitable.

Sometimes the question is posed, if Lenin had lived, could he have saved the situation? He may have had the authority to clarify that

Stalin's arguments, which flowed from the ideology of socialism in one country, were a break with Marxism. Lenin may have won more support in the Comintern and defeated the reactionary policies adopted towards the international opportunities that arose. Stalin made great play of Trotsky's late decision to join the Bolsheviks. But without a successful revolution somewhere else, if he were to remain faithful to the traditions he had built up in the Bolsheviks, Lenin would have had to tread the path taken by Trotsky: intransigent opposition to Stalin and a fight to keep alive the genuine traditions of workers' revolution. And this Trotsky and his followers did. This was no insignificant feat. Tens of thousands of them suffered and perished in Stalin's gulags.[158]

In countries where they opposed the local CPs, they were hounded, branded "Trotsky-fascists", even physically attacked at times to isolate them in the workers' movement. Whatever mistakes they made, in spite of their inability to change the course of history driven by Stalin, this contribution to revolutionary Marxism remains one of the most inspiring achievements of the movement. Their sacrifice, their determination to stand by the fundamental ideas of Marxism and to defend the interests of the working class, kept alive the central tenet of Marxism: that international workers' self-emancipation is the only basis for socialism. They kept alive what not just the Stalinists, but every capitalist and their hangers-on want to see snuffed out.[159]

Chapter nine
Was there a more peaceful, parliamentary alternative?

THERE ARE HISTORIANS WHO ARGUE that the Bolsheviks instigated a violent civil war, and that if they had wanted it, there could have been a peaceful, parliamentary compromise. The argument is based partly on the assertions about October being a coup which we've dealt with, but also on the notion that the Bolsheviks could have formed a democratic, broad-based coalition government. Their dispersal of the Constituent Assembly in January 1918 is presented as evidence that they deliberately turned their back on a peaceful, democratic outcome. With the turn to the right in recent historiography these arguments have become more widespread, and have even won the support of historians such as Eric Hobsbawm who previously was a supporter of the revolution. This is part of the fallout from the collapse of the Stalinist bloc. Those who thought those regimes were either socialist, or on their way to it, dealt with that collapse by disowning not just Stalin, but the revolution itself. Hobsbawm asks: "What made the Bolsheviks decide to take power with an obviously unrealistic program of socialist revolution?" and dismisses the hoped-for revolution in Germany as a "myth".[160]

Let's look at some facts. Firstly, the "mythical" German Revolution and the unrealistic prospect of international revolution. The German Revolution had all the features of Russia – workers' and soldiers' councils and a struggle for power between the capitalist and working classes. The revolutionary situation was not resolved until 1923 with the defeat of the workers' movement in October. Soviet governments briefly took power in Hungary and Bavaria. In Austria the monarchy was destroyed by a workers' revolution. France was swept by a revolutionary revolt, and the British government put the army on alert, so threatened did they feel during 1919 by the upsurge of working-class militancy. Mass factory occupations in Italy in the *Bienno Rosso* (Two Red Years) of 1919-20 raised the hope of revolution. And as far away as Australia and the US workers were inspired to talk of revolution, even setting up a soviet briefly in Seattle.

Secondly the truth about the anti-democratic brutality of the capitalist class both in Russia and internationally rarely sullies the texts of those seeking to blame the Bolsheviks for the civil war and its bloodshed. Victor Serge began his life as a libertarian revolutionary, and only after his experience of the Russian Revolution critically supported the Bolsheviks. In the most difficult circumstances – suffering serious illness, and living in the midst of Stalin's terror in 1928, he wrote down what he knew of revolutionary Russia. He left a chilling reminder of what the alternative to workers' power and the Bolshevik government actually was.

In Moscow, on 28 October 1917, when workers' organisations were just taking over the city's main institutions, a commander guarding the Kremlin surrendered to Junkers. He had been given a solemn promise that his men's lives would be spared, that "order had been restored". They were massed in a courtyard when suddenly the covers were ripped off machine guns. Serge quotes one of them who survived:

> [T]he men still cannot believe that they are going to be shot like this, without trial, without sense – they have taken no part in the fighting. A command bellows out: "In line now! Eyes front!" The men stand rigid, fingers along the seams of their trousers. At a signal, the din of the three machine guns blends with cries of terror, sobs and death-rattles. All those who are not mown down by the first shots dash towards the only exit, a little door behind them which has been left open. The machine-guns carry on firing; in a few minutes the doorway is blocked by a heap of men, lying there screaming and bleeding, into which the bullets still ram... The walls of the surrounding buildings are spattered with blood and bits of flesh.

Serge goes on:

> [T]his massacre is not an isolated act. Practically everywhere the Whites conducted arrests followed by executions... Let us remember these

facts. They show the firm intention of the defenders of the provisional government to drown the workers' revolution in blood. The White terror had begun.[161]

And it continued mercilessly in cities and villages wherever the Whites got the upper hand, but there was "nothing to compare in horror with what took place in Finland". From the earliest days of the civil war where the Finnish Whites were in control, "membership of a workers' organisation meant arrest, and any office in one meant death by shooting". Serge writes that "the massacre of the socialists reached such a scale that people lost all interest in the topic". At Rauma, Kummen, Kotka, in Helsinki – hundreds at a time, often with no identification, were summarily executed. Red Guards were hunted down from house to house and many women were among the victims. At Sveaborg public executions were carried out by the Whites on Trinity Sunday. Near Lahti, where thousands of prisoners were taken, "the machine-guns worked for several hours each day. In one day some 200 women were shot with explosive bullets: lumps of flesh were spattered out in all directions". At Viipuri 600 Red Guards were lined up in three rows along the edge of the fortress moat and machine-gunned in cold blood.

No real statistics exist, but estimates when Serge was writing were that between ten and twenty thousand were massacred. However there were official records of the number of Red (i.e. Bolshevik) prisoners interned in concentration camps: 70,000.

> The camps were ravaged by famine, vermin and epidemic. A report signed by a well-known Finnish doctor...notes that "between 6 July and 31 July 1918...in the camp at Tummerfors...2,347 prisoners died and the weekly mortality rate among detainees was as high as 407 per thousand".

Serge considered it no exaggeration to declare the total number of workers struck down by the Whites in Finland (i.e. killed or imprisoned for long periods) was more than 100,000, about a quarter of the entire proletariat. One group of Finnish Communists wrote at the beginning of 1919 that "all organised workers have been either imprisoned or shot".[162]

This ferocity towards the revolutionary masses had deep roots in the prejudices and material interests of the capitalist ruling class. Lord Charles Hardinge, the permanent Undersecretary of State for Foreign Affairs of Great Britain, in a letter to Sir George Buchanan, the British Ambassador in Petrograd in April 1917, summed up the general attitude to democracy, and consequently to the Russian Revolution, by the international bourgeoisie:

> How I hate the word democracy at the present time: if we do not win the war, as it should be won, it will be thanks to the Russian revolution and the absurd nonsense talked about the democracies of the world.[163]

Yes, these facts are horrendous, difficult to confront, so grotesque as to be unbelievable. But believe them we must, because they need to be burned into our consciousness. This is the nature of the class who rule over us. They may seem civilised when their system is going along without too much challenge to their power. But this barbarity was the alternative to workers' power. Because as Serge observed:

> [T]he terror is in reality the result of a calculation and a historical necessity. The victorious propertied classes are perfectly aware that they can only ensure their own domination in the aftermath of a social battle by inflicting on the working class a bloodbath savage enough to enfeeble it for tens of years afterwards. And since the class in question is far more numerous than the wealthy classes, the number of victims *must* be great.[164]

By at least August 1917, the capitalist class and their reactionary backers were determined that there would be no democracy in Russia if they had their way. Those who argue that the Bolsheviks cut off a road to parliamentary democracy which would have avoided the problems the Soviet regime encountered ignore this fact. The belief that this option existed as an alternative outcome of the revolution is utopian. It ignores the nature of dual power. One power or the other has to assert its unchallenged authority. And the reactionaries could see that for their side to gain that kind of control they would have to use brute force, because any democratic expression by the masses would mean support for the enemies of capitalism. In their eyes the enemy was simply the Bolsheviks. From July on, they referred to "Bolshevik Petrograd" like a code, signifying evil incarnate, and it was the symbol of all that justified their conspiracies for a military dictatorship.

Bolshevik attempts at compromise

After the Kornilov rebellion, the Bolsheviks offered a compromise with the provisional government. They would not agitate to overthrow the government if it agreed to implement some of the basic demands of the workers and peasants and prepare for peace. But the government, including the moderate socialists who had joined it, refused. Then, with astounding audacity, after the successful October insurrection, they clamoured for the Bolsheviks to compromise with their opponents in the Soviet. Trotsky was scathing in his speech to the All-Russian Congress of Soviets:

> The masses of the people followed our banner and our insurrection was victorious. With whom ought we compromise? With whom? With those wretched groups who have left us [they had walked out of the Congress] or who are making this proposal? But after all we've had a full view of them. No one in Russia is with them any longer. A compromise is supposed to be made, as between two equal sides, by the millions of workers and peasants represented in this congress, whom they are ready, not for the first time or the last, to barter away as the bourgeoisie sees fit. No, here no compromise is possible... [W]e must say "you are miserable bankrupts, your role is played out, go where you ought to go into the dustbin of history!"[165]

Trotsky and the Bolsheviks were not the only ones who understood that the masses were with them, that the insurrection was not a coup, but the expression of the will of the vast majority of the downtrodden and oppressed. Even the Cadet leader Miliukov wrote later:

> General dissolution [of Russia] began under the provisional government... The disorganisation resulting from the extraordinary military effort, the extreme lassitude of the army, the economic disarray, all this prepared

Russia for the Bolshevism... Lenin had only to sanction an accomplished fact to assure the sympathy of the soldiers, peasants and workers."[166]

And yet there are always those who argue that the Bolshevik government was illegitimate. From the days of preparation for the Kornilov coup, there is no mistaking the intentions of the provisional government and its supporters – and it wasn't democracy, or a compromise with the Bolsheviks. Take the plan to put General Krymov in charge of the operation in Petrograd. He was described by that arch-reactionary General Denikin as "full of the joy of life". But Kornilov made clear that it was a selective love of life, and for this very reason, Krymov was the one Kornilov trusted with his plans for the death of the popular revolution: "I am convinced that he will not hesitate, if need arises, to hang the whole membership of the Soviet of Workers' and Soldiers' Deputies".[167]

Kornilov also organised a plan by which Krymov would liquidate the revolutionary Kronstadt Soviet. Krymov was to send an artillery brigade to the coast nearby and, under the resultant bombardment from the shore, he was to demand that the Kronstadt garrison disarm the fortress and transfer themselves to the mainland. There, the sailors were to undergo mass executions.[168]

In the first few days after the fall of the tsar, the representatives of the old ruling classes were already preparing for the total destruction of workers' democracy. From the start they saw that the alternative could well be military dictatorship, and they did not flinch from that prospect. On the morning of 27 February, when the deputies from the Duma, the old tsarist parliament, learned that it had been dissolved, the left-leaning Cadet Nekrasov proposed "to establish a military dictatorship, handing over the whole power to a popular general".[169] John Reed in *Ten Days that Shook the World* testified to the absolute absence of democratic principles driving the capitalist class in its determination to end the situation of dual power in their own favour. In the words of the "Russian Rockefeller", a prominent Cadet:

> As for the Bolsheviki, they will be done away with by one of two methods. The government can evacuate Petrograd, then a state of siege declared, and the military commander of the district can deal with these gentlemen

without legal formalities ... Or if, for example, the Constituent Assembly manifests any Utopian tendencies, it can be dispersed by force of arms.[170]

The counter-revolutionaries had absolutely no interest in democracy, truthfulness or any shred of human decency. They blatantly manufactured hysterical myths about German gold arriving for the Bolsheviks. Miliukov, who strutted around as a professional historian, wrote in his history that such resources arrived for Trotsky "exactly in this period" to "prove" that there was an imminent insurrection being hatched by the Bolsheviks. Little does he care that all of the Bolsheviks' efforts were being directed towards *preventing* an insurrectionary uprising from mid-July until Kornilov's uprising at the end of August, nor does he think it relevant to mention that Trotsky was languishing in jail from 23 July until 4 September.

Employing what would during the century become standard practice by great powers in their dealings with mass movements they wished to destroy, the only insurrection on the drawing board was the one by Cossack Colonel Dutov, who admitted in January 1918: "I was to take action in the form of a Bolshevik insurrection". This was to be the pretext for the military assault on the capital.[171]

But then there are the other socialist groups. Did the Bolsheviks refuse to form a coalition with them because they wanted to form their own dictatorship? Hobsbawm and others think they should have and could have formed a "broad coalition with other socialists". Again, let's look at the facts. At the Soviet Congress the Bolsheviks clearly offered the hand of compromise to their opponents in spite of Trotsky's rhetoric. First they willingly voted for a motion by the Left Menshevik Martov calling for a peace conference to settle the disagreements. One by one, the Right stood on the podium to hurl insults and threats at the assembled delegates, declaring that the Congress had no authority, that they refused to take any responsibility for the defence of the new regime, blatantly declaring their solidarity with the counter-revolution and absolute hostility to not just the Bolsheviks, but to soviet power.

> The Right Mensheviks declare "the impossibility of work in collaboration with the Bolsheviks". One after another, the right and compromising

factions walk out of the Congress. If they cannot command a majority, they will not participate. They refuse to stand with the victors of this revolution to which they had declared their support – as long as they had the majority. As the Socialist Revolutionary, Karelin, said from the podium "the Bolsheviks are not to blame for their withdrawal."[172]

In any case there were talks between the Bolsheviks and the other socialists about forming a coalition government. And the evidence does not indicate that it was the Bolsheviks who ensured their failure. Apart from their demand that the government *exclude* the Bolsheviks – hardly a coalition of all forces – the actions and words of the moderate socialists all point to a determination to ensure there was no coalition with the Bolsheviks. Gendelman, who led the SRs out of the Congress, told the Committee for Salvation "even in the democratic camp there are moments when it is necessary to decide an agreement with weapons". When it became clear that this proclamation of intent coincided with an attempted coup by Cadet army officers under the flag of the Committee, the Railway Union, which had been brokering the discussions, expressed their disgust. They condemned not just the right, but those in the centre who were determined to cooperate with them as "the madmen who at this moment...do not want compromise... quite unconcerned for the consequences". A Marxist historian of the revolution insists:

> [T]he talks crumbled not because of an objection in principle to a socialist coalition on the part of the Bolshevik leadership but because the SRs and Mensheviks were not prepared to negotiate a meaningful coalition, and because, as they prevaricated, their own side was falling apart.[173]

Trotsky's attacks on the compromisers provide an explanation of why they refused the coalition and also answers their accusation that the Bolsheviks pre-empted a democratic transfer of power to the soviets:

> These socialists and democrats, having made a compromise by hook and crook with the imperialist bourgeoisie, today flatly refuse to compromise with the people in revolt.[174]

> Openly and before the face of the whole people we raised the banner of insurrection. The political formula of this insurrection was: All power to the soviets – through the Congress of Soviets. They tell us: You did not await the Congress with your uprising. We thought of waiting, but Kerensky would not wait. The counter-revolutionists were not dreaming. We as a party considered this our task: to make it genuinely possible for the Congress of Soviets to seize the power. If the Congress had been surrounded with Junkers, how could it have seized the power?[175]

However, the Bolsheviks were able to form a coalition government with the Left SRs, partly because the SRs were fundamentally divided and the Left SRs were forced to form their own party.

> Before the workers of Russia open new horizons which history has never known... [this workers' movement] is international... The old world crumbles down, the new world begins.

So proclaimed Maria Spiridonova, leader of the Left Socialist Revolutionary Party – "the most loved and the most powerful woman in all Russia" according to John Reed – two weeks after the October Revolution of 1917. She was addressing a triumphal meeting of several thousand delegates in the Russian capital Petrograd, celebrating the formation of their revolutionary government of Bolsheviks and Left SRs based on the soviets of workers, soldiers and peasants.

The Constituent Assembly

The Constituent Assembly, elected in November, assembled on 5 January 1918, but was dispersed because it was a centre that the counter-revolution hoped to use as an organising base against the Soviet regime. Opponents of the revolution, and even some who have written sympathetic accounts such as Rex Wade, think this is a clear-cut argument: the Bolsheviks refused to allow a democratically-elected parliament to exist, proving that they were intent on their own dictatorship. Wade even says this was the reason civil war became inevitable.[176]

To understand what's wrong with these arguments we need to interrogate the question of the nature of democracy, and then consider some facts. Lenin explained in *Pravda* that parliamentary democracy is the highest form of democracy in capitalist society. And so socialists demand it, support it, and defend it against dictatorship. However, the soviets and factory committees are the democratic forms of a workers' state and therefore a much higher form of democracy – and the only one that ensures the transition to socialism.[177] This was not a mere self-justification by Lenin, but is an important Marxist proposition. Rosa Luxemburg, combating proposals for a constituent assembly in Germany after the creation of workers' councils in November 1918, spelled it out in *Die Rote Fahne*, the paper of her organisation, the Spartacists:

> The choice today is not between democracy and dictatorship. The question which history has placed on the agenda is: *bourgeois* democracy or *socialist* democracy. For the dictatorship of the proletariat is democracy in the socialist sense of the term. The dictatorship of the proletariat ... means using every means of political power to construct socialism, to expropriate the capitalist class, in agreement with and by the will of the revolutionary majority of the proletariat, in the spirit of socialist democracy. Without the conscious will and the conscious activity of the majority of the proletariat, there can be no socialism. A class organisation [meaning the workers' councils] is needed to sharpen this consciousness, to organise this activity: the parliament of the proletarians of town and country.[178]

As we have seen, the soviets, factory committees, trade unions and other grassroots organisations were the means by which the masses could assert their political and social power. "The soviets are ours!" was the sentiment at the time. Luxemburg's passionate defence of these expressions of mass political power generalised the theoretical understanding of Marxism from the workers' experience and confirmed that the Bolsheviks were right to defend the soviets against the attempts to establish the Constituent Assembly as a rival power base.

The Constituent Assembly was an organising centre for the exploiters and their supporters. A Committee for the Defence of the

Constituent Assembly was composed only of intellectuals divorced from the mass of workers and soldiers. All those who rail against the Bolsheviks for organising an insurrection are less vocal about the plans of the Bolsheviks' "socialist" enemies. An SR terrorist outfit was organised to kidnap or assassinate Trotsky and Lenin. This plan was abandoned for fear the disappearance of such prominent leaders would cause a backlash of momentous proportions. Nevertheless two of the terrorists did attempt to kill Lenin. A demonstration planned for the opening of the Assembly "was both numerous and pathetic... attended *en masse* by the petty-bourgeois" according to Victor Serge.[179]

The composition of the Assembly is often taken as evidence that the Bolsheviks did not command the majority support they liked to assume. However, numerous historians have shown that if the SR vote is assessed in light of the mass support for the Lefts, a fact not allowed for in the listing of the parties, the Bolsheviks and Left SRs would have had a majority. One historian who studied Saratov province found that peasants there complained that they had voted for the SRs under duress and wanted to change to the Bolsheviks because they supported their land decree. The Bolsheviks got 25 percent, and the Left SRs had a majority of the 40 percent the SRs won, making the revolutionary parties who did form a coalition government the majority.[180]

However, regardless of the actual votes, a bourgeois parliament is never as reflective of the masses and the system never as accountable as the soviets. It could not serve the interests of the minority ruling class if it was. In any case it is indisputable that the fuss over the Constituent Assembly is one manufactured by historians after the event in order to bolster the arguments against the Bolsheviks. At the time, its passing was anything but an issue amongst the population except for the minority who supported the counter-revolution. Even the story of its "dispersal" is comical, reflecting its true standing. The Bolsheviks had already announced their intention of withdrawing and left. At about 4am, after the Left SRs had also withdrawn, the chair was interrupted by one of the soldiers on duty to guard the meeting. To the amazement of this self-important reactionary gathering, the soldier instructed the chair: "The guards are tired. Please leave the hall". To chants of "that's enough!" from the gallery the delegates quickly passed a few resolutions and wound up the business. Serge ends his narrative with "the dissolution of the Constituent Assembly made a great sensation abroad. In Russia, it passed almost unnoticed".[181]

To defend the Constituent Assembly is to defend the attempts of the capitalist class to stamp their will on a population entirely against the will of the vast majority. If you accept this argument, you have to accept that socialism is not possible, because the capitalist class will always try to counterpose their political system to that of a workers' state. Germany 1918–23 was a clear example of that.[182] The two different forms of democracy cannot be reconciled because they are the basis for organising society in completely different ways. This explains why historians like Hobsbawm turned to the argument about the Constituent Assembly to explain what went wrong. After decades of arguing that the Stalinist state was some form of socialism, when it collapsed they gave up on any hope for socialism. The argument that the Bolsheviks should have conceded the right of the capitalists to their centre of power in the Constituent Assembly fits nicely with the pessimism of those who abandoned any commitment to socialism after the collapse of the Stalinist monolith. It is an acceptance that capitalist political structures are sacrosanct.

On the question of a free press we need a similar approach: there are different class interests battling it out to determine whether society will be based on the exploitation and competition of capitalism, or go forward to a society based on collectivism and production for human need. Opponents of the workers' state always oppose the suppression of the counter-revolutionary capitalist-owned press. But this ignores the fact that the only alternatives left were workers' power or a military coup. The only question was: which side are you on? The press the Bolsheviks closed down was run by those who had violently smashed Bolshevik printing presses from July up until October. Freedom for the counter-revolutionary press meant freedom to organise for the likes of Guchkov, a capitalist and the first minister of war in the provisional government. We saw how he and some of the major capitalists such as AI Putilov, with the cooperation of banks and insurance companies masquerading as the "Society for the Economic Rehabilitation of

Russia" set up a fund they put "at the disposal of Kornilov for the purposes of organising an armed struggle against the Soviets".

So contrary to wishful thinking by the revolution's enemies, or by utopians who think socialism can be wished into existence, there was not some happy compromise between all parties on offer that the Bolsheviks wilfully crushed so they could rule on their own. The other "socialist" parties, which had increasingly thrown in their lot with the capitalists, refused to participate in a purely Soviet government. Their conditions included only minority representation for the Bolsheviks, who clearly commanded a majority in the workers' soviets, and the exclusion of their leading members Lenin and Trotsky. How democratic is that?

But for those who still harbour doubts about the Bolsheviks' true motives, and who suspect that with good will a more peaceful outcome could have been achieved, they should look at the German Revolution of 1918-23. It was crushed by the state with the backing of the Social Democratic Party (SPD) – a party with the same kind of politics as the compromisers in Russia. The leadership of the German Communist Party were murdered with the active backing of the SPD, the workers' democracy was destroyed and thousands of workers massacred in the name of capitalist "law and order", all supported and in part carried out by the SPD.[183] It is significant that Hobsbawm dismisses this revolution as a "myth", because to study it is to throw light on the Russian experience. This is not just a question of the Bolsheviks and their particular theory, or the nature of their organisation. It is a question of social forces and the class struggle. Pierre Broué, in his magnificent history of the German Revolution, sums up the social forces which mirrored those, albeit with their differences, of Russia:

> The fact is that, despite its [initial] defeat, the German bourgeoisie... had at its disposal an instrument of rare quality, the officer corps, and above all the total support of the flexible, experienced apparatus of Social Democracy, which would know how to defend effectively what it called "order" against "chaos", and "freedom" against "dictatorship". It confirmed Liebknecht's warning on 10 November by finally enabling the positions of the counter-revolution to triumph within the very heart of the councils.

Finally, the German bourgeoisie enjoyed the solid support of the armies of the Entente, the threatening shadow of which hung over this whole period of the German Revolution.[184]

The coalition government of the Bolsheviks and the Left SRs sued for an end to World War I, scandalised the bourgeois world by publishing secret treaties between the Allies, and began putting workers in control of their factories. It was a beacon of freedom for the workers of the world and remains so. Those who claim the October Revolution was a coup that derailed the impetus towards parliamentary democracy ignore the ruthless intent of those who were determined that workers would not rule. And they dismiss the most significant action by the mass of oppressed and exploited classes in the history of humanity.

It is fitting to leave the revolution with the words of Trotsky, to emphasise the immensity of the achievements of the Russian workers, and their creativity and organising genius that the revolution revealed: "The Revolution is before and above all the awakening of humanity".

Chapter ten
The relevance of 1917 for today

THE 1917 RUSSIAN REVOLUTION STANDS AS A REMINDER that a better world was and is possible. The working class in Russia was a tiny minority in a mostly peasant population. Today workers are the majority in virtually every country and are more literate, cultured and highly educated. So if Russian workers could defeat the capitalist class, so can we. News of the revolution spread like wildfire, inspiring movements of resistance and support. In Germany "the term 'workers' councils [*Arbeiterräte*]', the German rendering of the Russian 'soviets', entered the vernacular. These were the signs of subterranean movements which were preparing revolutionary explosions".[185] In 1917 workers often only found out the truth many months later from seamen carrying news that combated lies in the capitalist press. Today, instead of weeks and months, it will take minutes for images and words to beam around the globe.

To understand the defeat of the revolution while preserving the inspiration and importance of the workers' heroic struggle, it is necessary to recognise that the Russian Revolution could not lay the basis for socialism without support from victorious workers' revolutions in at least some of the most advanced capitalist countries. But one of the important and enduring lessons that needs to be imprinted on the brains of all those who wonder about the virtue of revolution as opposed to reform is the role of those moderate "socialists" – the likes of today's ALP – who claimed they were for the masses, but who ended up supporting the counter-revolution. These two questions are inextricably linked. The role of the German SPD, a carbon copy of the treachery of the compromisers in Russia, even further undermines the arguments of those who would have us believe that the bloodshed of the civil war in Russia was the fault of the Bolsheviks.

The Bolsheviks did not invoke the international revolution as simply a mantra, they put serious effort into building a new Communist International to try to educate the newly radicalised organisations, and to group together the genuinely revolutionary sections of them. They had to do this while at the same time fighting a bitter civil war in which the Whites, or counter-revolutionary forces, received massive military, economic and political backing from the Western Allies.[186] Against incredible odds, under Trotsky's leadership, a new, Red Army was established and the determination, perseverance and dedication of millions of workers and peasants finally defeated the counter-revolutionary Whites by 1921. But at a terrible cost.

By 1921, the wave of revolutions that had swept Europe had been forced into retreat, often by brute force from the reordered capitalist state. Within Russia itself the Bolsheviks expected to be defeated by an outright counter-revolution that would throw them out of power. But the victory in the civil war seemed to defy that. The counter-revolution from within their own ranks is able to be interpreted as though there is an unbroken continuity between the Bolsheviks under Lenin and Trotsky and the CPSU of Stalin's rule. This has led most historians, both hostile and sympathetic, to look for the seeds of Stalin's dictatorship in the ideas and political practice of Lenin. However, there are fundamental problems with this method, problems which, as argued above, obscure the actual reasons for the defeat. This is of critical importance if the Russian Revolution and the sacrifice by millions of workers that it entailed is to be honoured as it deserves. In order to give lasting meaning to the struggles of those masses it is imperative that the correct lessons are learnt so that their legacy contributes to the overthrow of capitalism.

The debate with Stalin over "socialism in one country" was not just a petty squabble, or a matter of pedantics among Marxists. Nor is it just an argument of historical interest with no relevance today. The defeat of the revolution and the debate over what happened created a dividing line on the left between the revolutionary actions and aspirations of 1917 and those who supported the new, monstrous state Stalin created in the name of Communism.

The argument that Stalin's regime was the logical outcome of Lenin and the Bolshevik Party's politics and program has led some on the left to accept the pessimistic view that the road to socialism involves bureaucratic, one-party states in which workers have virtually no rights. So repressive regimes – from Eastern Europe after World War II, to China, Cuba, Vietnam, North Korea and some in Africa – have been able to parade as communists, besmirching the vision of socialism and the human liberation it stands for, cheered on by most of the Western left. Apologists for these repressive states have blurred the lines between workers' power and the genuine struggle for socialism with labels such as "deformed workers' states" to refer to countries where no workers' revolution even took place. Or the Stalinist regimes have been pronounced to be "socialist oriented" while they deny any vestige of workers' control or democracy.

In 1917 it was an absolute necessity to clarify how workers could win their just demands. The arguments about what the options were for the great mass of workers and peasants in the situation of dual power are as relevant today as then. Because those who are not clear what they're fighting for don't just end up with some lesser compromise when revolutionary upheavals erupt. They end up on the other side of the barricades, as did the Russian compromisers of 1917 and the German SPD, who butchered the flower of the revolutionary proletariat.

Just as relevant today are the conclusions we draw about how to prepare for a future revolution. The idea that there was a straight line from Lenin to Stalin can lead to the conclusion that workers could and should take power, but they should do so without a party like the Bolsheviks leading the struggles. However, the history of the revolutions around Europe from 1917 to 1923 irrevocably proves how difficult the overthrow of the capitalist state and its replacement with a soviet regime is. And the missing link was everywhere the presence of a revolutionary organisation that had some understanding of what to do. Broué is explicit about the reason for the defeat in Germany:

> The drama and historic weakness of the German workers' and soldiers' councils is ultimately bound up with the fact that there did not exist a real "conciliar party", to encourage and invigorate them, and to take part in the

struggle for conciliar power, which the Bolsheviks were able to do between February and October 1917 ... confusion [among the revolutionaries] and the absence of a revolutionary organisation to lead a consistent struggle for winning the majority in the councils for the seizure of state power by the councils, left the field clear for the enemies of the councils who were at work within them.[187]

A revolutionary party needs years of preparation, because it needs to test its leaders, it needs to have developed a layer of cadre who have been steeled and educated in tactics and strategies, they need to have experienced the difficulties of being on the offensive without losing their heads, and also the virtue of patience when the working class is on the defensive. In other words, theory and practice can only be brought together in the process of building an organisation out of the day-to-day struggles of the masses. It cannot be constructed by an act of will, or by simply learning theory; and neither can it be cohered in a few weeks once the revolution has begun to unfold. Even where there were great revolutionaries just as talented and determined as Lenin, such as Rosa Luxemburg and Karl Liebknecht in Germany, they could not cohere the most advanced and class-conscious militants in the working class quickly enough in the turmoil of revolution.

The Russian Revolution of 1917 confirms all of the basic propositions of Marxism: that socialism will only be possible after the self-emancipation of the working class, and that the working class is capable of it. It confirms that the existing capitalist state must be destroyed, and that it must be replaced by a workers' state. In order to achieve that, the working class needs a party made up of the most class conscious, dedicated and determined workers who have considered these questions for years, and have incorporated them into their practice.

The Russian Revolution stands as a beacon that shines across the decades. It shows what is possible. Its defeat, rather than proving that it is pointless struggling for a socialist world, proves another fundamental tenet of Marxism: socialism cannot be built in one country. In order for a workers' state to transform society and liberate humanity, the revolution must be international. That means the presence of revolutionary organisations in other countries may be the decisive factor in ultimate victory or defeat. It certainly was after 1917. If revolutionary workers' parties can be built anywhere in the world on the basis of these lessons, then the tragedy of the Russian working class will not be in vain; their suffering will be honoured. Their short-lived victory can yet be repeated and extended in the twenty-first century.

Gender, class and the Bolsheviks[1]

If future historians look for the group that began the Russian Revolution, let them not create any involved theory. The Russian Revolution was begun by hungry women and children demanding bread and herrings. They started by wrecking tram cars and looting a few small shops. Only later did they, together with workmen and politicians, become ambitious to wreck that mighty edifice the Russian autocracy.[2]

By providing, almost by accident, a large-scale instance of unpunished civil disorder, they [the working-class women of Petrograd] demonstrated the hopeless inability of the government to preserve law and order at the centre of its power.[3]

On 23 February 1917 (8 March by the Western calendar), many thousands of angry working-class women in the Vyborg district of Petrograd, the centre of working-class radicalism and militancy, celebrated International Working Women's Day (IWD) by walking out on strike and flooding into the streets. The tsarina, wife of Tsar Nicholas II, dismissed their protest as "a hooligan movement", informing Nicholas that "if the weather was cold they would probably stay at home".[4]

The women marched to nearby workplaces where better organised and experienced male workers might be expected to come out

---

1. This chapter is based on research conducted after this book's first appearance. It was originally published as "Russia 1917: Gender, class and the Bolsheviks" in *Marxist Left Review* 14, Winter 2017. –*Ed.*
2. Sorokin 1950, p.3.
3. Stites 1990, p.290.
4. Harris 2017.

in solidarity. A worker in the Nobel engineering plant recalled a typical scene:

> We could hear women's voices in the lane... "Down with high prices!" "Down with hunger!" "Bread for the workers!" I and several comrades rushed at once to the windows... The gates of No 1 Bol'shaia Sampsonievskaia mill were flung open. Masses of women workers in a militant frame of mind filled the lane. Those who caught sight of us began to wave their arms, shouting: "Come out!" "Stop work!" Snowballs flew through the windows. We decided to join the demonstration.[5]

By the end of the day over 100,000, a third of the city's industrial workforce, were on strike.[6] The next day, meetings, proclamations, marches continued, the numbers on strike swelling to 200,000.

In other circumstances, this would be a not unusual narrative of the Russian workers' movement: strikers march around factories "calling out" other workers, who almost invariably join the protest in solidarity. But what followed has turned a spotlight on these events.

Five days later the Romanov autocracy of over 300 years had been trampled under the feet of these "hooligans" who had won the sympathy of the soldiers. They were backed up by virtually the entire workforce of Petrograd followed by Moscow. Their rebellion spread like wildfire to other urban centres, across the fertile plains, the frozen tundras, the mountainous Caucasus of the Russian empire. Nicholas, in a humiliating scene in a stranded railway car 300 kilometres south of Petrograd, was forced to abdicate by his own generals. They were frightened out of their wits, because their armed forces had stripped them and the tsar of their power.

The February Revolution: the question of spontaneity

There are several themes and interpretations entwined around the IWD strikes which deserve a critical eye. The women's actions are often portrayed as elemental, unorganised and apolitical. And so it was quite accidental that they sparked the revolution. This theme

---

5. Smith 1987, p.61.
6. Wade 2000, p.31.

strengthens the myth that this was a genuine, supportable revolution of the people, whereas October was nothing but a Bolshevik coup. As the feminist historians Jane McDermid and Anna Hillyar comment in their very useful book *Midwives of the Revolution*, "it is the image of an elemental force of women workers and their contribution to the social chaos of 1917 that underwrites the mirror image of the Bolsheviks as arch manipulators and usurpers of the popular movement".[7]

Students are asked, was the February Revolution "spontaneous", or was it "organised"? And if the latter, who led it? The question is based on the assumption that "spontaneity" and "organisation" are counterposed. But this does not help clarify the issue, it only confuses it. What is meant by organisation? Preparations and planning, or the existence of political organisations? Many discussions only consider the latter; and the political organisations were not the initiators of the February revolution, taking some time to catch up with events.

I think there is generally too much emphasis on the aspect of spontaneity in February, and this is linked to attitudes to women. Accounts which emphasise women's unplanned spontaneity downplay the role of leadership, foresight and planning by the women themselves. After all, it was organised textile workers who began it all. Tony Cliff, the Marxist biographer of Lenin, says "[t]he revolution was completely spontaneous and unplanned".[8] At the end of his discussion of this spontaneous revolution, Cliff says that actually the Bolshevik cadre provided the necessary leadership. But this is unhelpful. It sidesteps the question of the leading role of wider layers of women.

Every revolution begins with an unexpected turn of events. But they usually don't provoke a flurry of historical analysis of this phenomenon of spontaneity. For example, the Marxist Chris Harman, writing about the Hungarian Revolution of 1956, describes very clearly how a peaceful demonstration spontaneously became a revolution when fired on by armed forces, with not one mention of spontaneity.[9]

---

7. McDermid and Hillyar 1999, p.7.
8. Cliff 2004, p.89.
9. Harman 1988, pp.124–30; the accounts of revolutions in Barker 2002 similarly do not theorise spontaneity when there is clearly an element of it.

The fact is, the events of February 1917 are far from just an outburst of spontaneous anger. The IWD demonstrations took place in an atmosphere of tension, class conflict and preparations based on the expectation that a revolution was virtually inevitable at some stage soon.

The year had begun with a mass strike on 9 January, the anniversary of the massacre of Petrograd workers on Bloody Sunday 1905. Around 40 percent of the Petrograd industrial workers, including many women, went out. On 26 January, 700 weavers struck in protest at the sacking of a woman. A strike by women textile workers in the Vyborg district, where IWD would begin, lasted a full month and another in January lasted five days. As early as December 1916, almost a thousand women had walked off their shift in a munitions store where they worked beside better-paid men, demanding a pay rise.[10] On 14 February, another major strike of 84,000 closed down more than 52 factories in the midst of fears by the middle class that there would be "clashes" at the reopening of the Duma (parliament). Rex Wade paints a picture of the "growing turmoil" of strikes and demonstrations spreading to other cities in his book *The Russian Revolution, 1917*. On 22 February, the day before IWD, the presence of 30,000 workers, locked out by management at the giant Putilov works, "inflamed tensions". Women from the plant demonstrated at food warehouses over food prices and a protest march to the city's political centre was prevented by police. Workers who met with Duma delegates warned that this might be the beginning of a big political movement and that "something very serious might happen".[11]

The narrative of the February Revolution could just as well begin with the strike the day before IWD. But it did not offer the mystique of women leading vast masses, an image which cuts against sexist stereotypes and therefore intrinsically more interesting than the preceding rash of mass strikes. However we view the chronology of events, it is not credible to think that in this context the IWD strikes were some elemental, apolitical outburst.

---

10. McDermid and Hillyar 1999, pp.140–41.
11. Wade 2000, p.29.

Women had been involved since mid-1915 in bread riots which were probably more classically spontaneous: expressions of sheer anger and frustration at the lack of food to feed hungry families. During the war large numbers of women were drawn into the workforce to replace men sent to the front. By 1917 women made up over half the labour force in Petrograd.[12] The metal factories were the most strategically important, producing for the war, and politically the most advanced, with traditions of militancy and radicalism which had not been seriously undermined by conscription because the workers' skills were in such demand. Women grew from 2.7 percent of the metal industry workforce in 1913 to 20.3 percent by 1917, though they remained predominantly unskilled.[13] During 1916, both female and male workers were increasingly restive. In the six months before the revolution, over a million worker-days were spent on strike in Petrograd, 75 percent of which were political.[14] At least some women were preparing for months before IWD in 1917, weighing up the odds, assessing their actions and options. By January 1917 the spies (who spent their time recording every sign of opposition) recognised women's readiness for action:

> [M]others of families, exhausted from the endless queues at the shops, suffering at the sight of their sick and half-famished children, at this moment are much closer indeed to revolution than are Mssrs Milyukov, Rodichev, and Co. [liberal politicians]; and of course are more dangerous because they constitute a mass of inflammable matter for which only a spark is sufficient to cause it to burst into flames.[15]

On 23 February, a police agent reported "the idea that an uprising is the only means to escape from the food crisis is becoming more and more popular among the masses".[16] And many of the political arguments, the initiative and foresight came from workers who had

---

12. McDermid and Hillyar 1999, p.128.
13. Smith 1983, p.24.
14. Mandel 1983, p.63.
15. Stites 1990, p.290.
16. Wade 2000, p.32.

already experienced the revolution of 1905 and the aftermath when it was crushed. They knew that certain things had to be prepared, such as winning the soldiers over. For instance, the factory worker Anastasia Deviatkina, who organised and led a demonstration on IWD, had been a Bolshevik member for 13 years.[17] Textile workers were in the habit of approaching the soldiers to persuade them not to attack protests. And a few days before IWD the largely female staff at the Vasilevsky Island trolley-car park sent a woman to the nearby regiment to ask the soldiers if they would fire on them if they came out. The soldiers' answer was no, ensuring that on IWD the trolley-car workers joined the demonstration. Women were participating in the preparations for the anticipated uprising, cognisant of the issues they faced.

On the 25th, 240,000 were now on strike and thousands of students joined their demonstrations. The soldiers were increasingly insubordinate. Their officers tried to use the age-old tactic of sexist put-downs, referring to the women approaching the troops as "old hags" and the like. But the women's heartfelt appeals to their common experience of suffering because of the war ate at the soldiers' hearts. Trotsky, in his magnificent book *The History of the Russian Revolution*, pays due tribute to the women and their role in winning over the soldiers:

> [W]omen...go up to the cordons more boldly than men, take hold of the rifles, beseech, almost command: "Put down your bayonets – join us". The soldiers are excited, ashamed, exchange anxious glances, waver...the bayonets rise guiltily above the shoulders of the advancing crowd. The barrier is opened, a joyous and grateful "Hurrah!" shakes the air...the revolution makes another forward step.[18]

On the question of spontaneity Trotsky sums up:

> The mystic doctrine of spontaneousness explains nothing. In order correctly to appraise the situation and determine the moment for a

---

17. McDermid and Hillyar 1999, p.151.
18. Trotsky 1977, p.129.

blow at the enemy...[i]t was necessary that throughout this mass should be scattered workers who had thought over the experience of 1905, criticised the constitutional illusions of the liberals and Mensheviks... meditated hundreds of times about the question of the army...workers capable of making revolutionary inferences from what they observed and communicating them to others...

Elements of experience, criticism, initiative, self-sacrifice, seeped down through the mass and created, invisibly to a superficial glance but no less decisively, an inner mechanics of the revolutionary movement as a conscious process. To the smug politicians... everything that happens among the masses is customarily represented as an instinctive process.[19]

And I think we can add that when women are involved this is even more pronounced. Rex Wade makes a perceptive observation:

[T]he disintegration of the discipline of the soldiers, reflecting the large number of new recruits and the antiwar sentiments of veterans and recruits alike, was one of the most important of the many unplanned, even spontaneous, aspects of the February Revolution.[20]

Could it be that others have not noticed this because the dominant image of spontaneous outbursts doesn't fit with the image of men in general and soldiers in particular?

There are not two counterposed phenomena: either leaderless spontaneity or organised workers leading the backward. There can be a mixture of conscious organising, conscious considerations and then somewhat unexpected, unpredictable, or "spontaneous" actions. While the IWD manifestation was not "planned" by the Bolsheviks, the largest of the socialist organisations – and the Mensheviks and Socialist Revolutionaries had no interest in IWD, only responding once the uprising was well underway – it was really not the spontaneous outburst many like to portray. Spontaneity and the drive to self-activity and organisation were really more a feature of the rest of 1917, reflected in

---
19. ibid., pp.169-71.
20. Wade 2000, p.34.

the plethora of organisations, such as the soviets (workers' councils), factory committees, Red Guards[21] and the like, which flourished after the uprising destroyed the monarchy.

Gender and class[22]

Social historian David Mandel has dealt with the issue of the place of women in the workforce in a detailed study of the Petrograd working class.[23] Women workers were very similar to unskilled male workers, with high levels of illiteracy, less secure employment and extremely low wages. But women had the added burden of their special oppression: family responsibilities, the difficulties of childbirth, lack of contraception, sexual harassment by foremen and bosses, plus society's and the church's promotion of the idea of the patriarchal household which encouraged their enslavement to the men in their lives. Mandel argues that:

> [T]he woman worker's life was a closed one, an almost unbroken passage between home and mill that kept her isolated from the larger society, outside the dynamic of the labour movement.
>
> The unskilled workers were the least active element of Petrograd's working class. In labour circles they were often referred to as the *malosoznatel'nye massy* (literally – masses with low consciousness) and sometimes merely *boloto* (the swamp).
>
> By far the largest single group in this category were the women. V Perazich, a Petrograd union activist, wrote of the textile workers: "Our masses in general at that time [early 1917] were still totally benighted... Only very few had managed to become conscious proletarians".[24]

---

21. Armed workers' militias organised in the factories and districts.
22. There is a large body of work on the revolution in which there is much information about the role of women and how their situation influenced their participation. Right-wing historians usually ignore them. Here, my purpose isn't to give a detailed account of their activities so much as to raise theoretical and political issues arising from some of the best feminist and social histories.
23. Mandel 1983, pp.23-33.
24. ibid., p.25.

Women were mostly employed at menial unskilled and semi-skilled work in textiles, food-processing, chemicals and shoemaking, or unskilled production jobs. However, Perazich comments on the increased number of women who replaced class conscious male workers in the war-related manufacturing workplaces: "It reached a point where women appeared even on the mules where they had never worked before, and among the women at this time there were still too few conscious workers".[25] So while not ignoring the specific oppression women suffered, Mandel makes an important point: "[I]t must be emphasised that it was not sex but the level of skill and the social characteristics associated with it in Russia that were the primary determinants of political culture".[26]

And the needle trades illustrate the point. A significant proportion of women did two to three years of training at schools or in apprenticeships; their overall literacy rate was 68.2 percent compared with 37.9 percent in cotton. Some seamstresses were urban-bred, daughters of workers. These skilled workers were quite unlike their unskilled sisters. Seven of eight textile workers interviewed in one study were raised in the village in peasant families. Interviewers described them as "downtrodden", "uncultured", "underdeveloped", "uninterested in public life"; while the seamstresses were perceived as "energetic", "intelligent", and "capable", noting that two of them were actively involved in public affairs. Mandel says:

> [I]ndeed, the relatively few skilled women workers bore a far greater resemblance to their skilled male counterparts than to the unskilled women. And the converse is also true: the unskilled men...were very similar to the unskilled women in both social background and political culture. And like the women, they were referred to by Mensheviks and Bolsheviks alike as "undeveloped", "backward", "of low consciousness".[27]

So women workers entered the fray of revolution on a different footing from male skilled metal workers, regarded as the vanguard, but on a

---
25. ibid., p.23.
26. ibid., p.40.
27. ibid., p.28.

very similar basis to unskilled male workers. McDermid and Hillyar confuse the issues surrounding political culture, leadership and sexism. And so they see the solidarity shown by male workers which turned a protest into a revolution in a negative light: "the traditional hierarchy of the labour movement reasserted itself, and reimposed the distinction between economic and political questions". But the issues of food scarcity, wages and the like were highly political issues in the context of the war. The Bolshevik slogan, "Land, Bread and Peace!", taken up by masses of people, is hardly evidence that "bread and butter issues were pushed aside" as they claim.[28]

More importantly, it was natural for the most experienced to lead. Mandel shows that in the early February days, a meeting of the workers of the main workshops of the NW Railroad, mostly male, decided to send a delegation to the most politically advanced, the Putilov workers, to see what they were doing before taking action themselves. In the Vyborg district, the workers of the James Beck Textile Mill traditionally sought aid and advice on economic and political matters from the nearby New Lessner Machine-construction Factory.

The fact that the women marched to the metal factories in the Vyborg shows how integrated into the traditions of the working class their activity was. For decades it had been common practice to call out other workplaces, even forcing workers out by picketing and more violent means when necessary. The Treugol'nik Rubber Factory in the Narva District, for example, with an overwhelmingly female and unskilled workforce, had never struck during its entire pre-1917 history except when "taken out" by the more active workers from the relatively nearby Putilov works. And this tradition ensured the women escalated their action without much trouble. Wade says of the events after 23 February:

> [E]specially important were the factory activists... Drawing on lengthy strike experience they quickly moved to the fore and provided the organizational skills and leadership for the demonstrations of the next few days. They organized the columns of workers as they marched from the

---

28. McDermid and Hillyar 1999, p.157.

factories and exhorted workers to demonstrate rather than simply going home. They gave impassioned speeches articulating worker grievances and demanding the overthrow of the regime. These activists helped organize the strike committees and other revolutionary organizations.[29]

These leaders, mostly male, but including Bolshevik women, brought to the movement important political steadiness born of years of experience. Many workers wanted to keep increasing the militancy in the streets. But Alexander Shlyapnikov, the most prominent Bolshevik leader in Petrograd at the time, urged workers to instead put their efforts towards drawing the soldiers into the struggle, a more political task which required more patience, but a critical one and one in which women played a vital role.[30] The question wasn't whether women would continue in the leadership, but whether the most advanced could convince the masses who had responded to the women's call to rise to new heights of rebellion and organisation.

Because class is the root cause of all oppression, in a revolution all oppressed groups find some of their number on either side of the class line. This seems such a basic question, but it is consistently ignored by historians, as they search for a classless identity of "women" and "feminism". An incident on 1 April illustrates how raw these class divisions among women were. Mainly female textile workers were demonstrating against the Provisional Government. According to Perazich, pro-government demonstrators – well-dressed women and men – jeered at them, calling them *"Bezulochnitsy!"* (trollops), "Illiterate rabble! Filthy scum!", "stockingless!", "uneducated riff raff!", "ignoble sluts!". Pelageia Romanovna retorted from the workers' side: "the hats you're wearing are made from our blood!" In an ensuing fight, the workers' banners were torn down and used to hit them, but the workers managed to tear the hats and hat pins from the ladies' heads, leaving them with scratched faces.[31]

When historians write about "feminism" and "women's issues" they often seem to lose a grip on reality. Rex Wade, who writes

---
29. Wade 2000, p.32.
30. ibid., p.37.
31. Mandel 1983, p.115.

eloquently about the institutions workers established, and of women's involvement in the organisational creativity which erupted after February, resorts to homilies and ill-informed comments when he turns to these issues. The activities of the bourgeois feminists, he writes, "were the purest expression of specifically women's aspirations and activism in 1917". These included, as well as the vote, pressuring the government for the right to be lawyers – when working-class and peasant women needed education in basic literacy! He comments that "socialist leaders were concerned with women as low-paid workers rather than as people with special gender concerns".[32] As though low pay was not a gender issue. It's as though working-class women's demands for an end to sexual harassment by foremen and bosses, for equal pay, for maternity leave, for provision for the sick and elderly, are not about "women's aspirations". But in fact they weren't just women's demands; working-class men fought for them beside the women with great vigour, unlike bourgeois feminists.

Opposition to the war drove women workers' revolt. But liberal, upper-class feminists supported it, agitating to fight on after the revolution. The state they hoped their class would rule over needed to prove its credentials on the war front if it were to play a role as an imperialist power which the Allies would take seriously. And there was the question of defending the territories of the old empire which would contribute to their wealth and power.

On 20 March, the feminists held a 40,000-strong demonstration in Petrograd which marched with banners demanding universal suffrage in the anticipated Constituent Assembly – but, crucially, carrying banners which read "War until Victory!". When the rally reached the headquarters of the Provisional Government, the Bolshevik leader Alexandra Kollontai tried to disrupt the speakers' platform by storming the stage and denouncing the feminists' support for the bloody horrors of the war and the uselessness of their demands. The outraged feminists pushed her off the platform, and some soldiers menaced her with their bayonets. But as might be expected, the crowd

---

32. Wade 2000, p.116–17.

started to divide; some of the soldiers who had been in the trenches were sympathetic to Kollontai, as well as some of the women, and they formed a group and marched off.[33] The feminists could not in any serious, ongoing way appeal to support among working-class women and soldiers' wives. They entertained the British suffragette Emmeline Pankhurst from June to September. Rabidly pro-war, she addressed private meetings in their mansions because the government worried that public forums by her would be met by protests. She helped raise money for a women's battalion to go to the front to replace the soldiers leaving in droves. It was these battalions who tried to defend the Winter Palace against the soviet insurrection in October. Workers didn't trust the government, so women workers could turn up to a rally demanding universal suffrage in any constituent assembly it might convene, but there was no genuine class unity even in this situation. Let's remember that women workers were voting and being elected in the factory committees, trade unions and soviets.

The role of the Bolsheviks

McDermid and Hillyar document the important role the Bolsheviks played in educating and involving women.[34] Yet they throw doubt in one way or another on their attitudes. There is always a qualification, a "but" or "although" which indicates a reluctance to accept the fact that there was no "pure" women's struggle, as Rex Wade puts it. They exhibit a squeamishness about admitting that it was only by class struggle with an orientation to uniting male and female workers that the rights of working-class women could seriously be put on the agenda.

Midwives of the Revolution is excellent in many respects. But throughout the book, the authors reveal a serious lack of understanding of the Bolsheviks' history, politics and methods. Unlike many of Alexandra Kollontai's biographers, they find it "interesting" that Lenin was one of the Bolsheviks who backed her attempts to organise working-class women against opposition from women leaders – presumably because it contradicts the mythology that Kollontai had to battle the male leadership to get support for organising among women.

---

33. Donald 1982; Stites 1990, p.293.
34. McDermid and Hillyar 1999, pp.143–54.

Richard Stites, the historian of women's liberation in Russia, says that Lenin "revealed an uncompromising adherence to political equality for women".[35] Lenin was often the one to initiate work among women. The first material the Social Democrats had for women, a pamphlet written in the 1890s by Krupskaya, Lenin's close collaborator (and wife), was his idea. And he put considerable effort into helping Krupskaya write it, providing her with information he had accumulated in his research for his work on the development of capitalism in Russia. In 1910 Lenin supported the idea of doing work among women émigrés. Then in 1913 he was instrumental in organising an editorial board for a working-class women's journal, *Rabotnitsa* (Woman Worker).

McDermid and Hillyar think it is "ironic" that while propagandising for working-class women's struggles, Kollontai was "the party's leading theoretical and political opponent of the feminist movement".[36] There was nothing ironic or contradictory about this. The feminist movement of the time was a class force based among liberal capitalist women and therefore opposed to most of the demands of the mass of women. So revolutionaries identified as Marxists, not feminists. The terminology of today, when "feminism" simply denotes for most people support for women's rights, confuses the issues when applied to this period.

Of course, there were debates and arguments among Bolsheviks. But this was not "feminists" vs male Bolsheviks as it's often portrayed. Kollontai and other women spoke at party meetings about women's right to work and the need to organise women into the unions. This is no different from any other question. There are always disagreements in revolutionary organisations, especially until an orthodoxy is established, and even then, new members have to be educated in it. Questions of the role of the intelligentsia, imperialism, war, were all subjects of debate. The question is, what did the leading members argue and what position was established? All of the women involved in organising working-class women were close collaborators

---

35. Stites 1990, p.237.
36. McDermid and Hillyar 1999, p.8. For a full assessment of Kollontai's role and the attitudes to her in the Bolsheviks, see my Note of March 2017, "Who Was Alexandra Kollontai?", https://www.facebook.com/notes/sandra-bloodworth/who-was-alexandra-kollontai/1305556992857977/.

of Lenin, indicating that he was part of a circle of leading Bolsheviks who took this work seriously.[37]

Because of inconsistencies it's not clear whether McDermid and Hillyar reject or just misunderstand the arguments about class, or whether they feel the need to make concessions to the identity politics so popular in the last few decades. However it is clear they do not grasp the dynamic of how struggles over economic demands can develop, or how the Bolsheviks related to them. For instance, they acknowledge that the Bolshevik Alexander Shlyapnikov was clear about the impact on women of the food shortages, high prices and having the men away fighting and dying. But they say "yet [he] still saw their actions and motivation as essentially apolitical, more a domestic reflection of war weariness than a sign of rising political awareness".[38] But Shlyapnikov, a long term leading member, would have been imbued with the Bolshevik approach, which was that immediate concrete demands over workers' conditions were the most likely catalyst for workers' struggle. And the experience of this struggle would develop political consciousness.[39]

However, the page reference in Shlyapnikov's memoirs they give covers his time in New York. Actually, when writing about the food crisis, he says: "All around revolutionary work was seething. All circles of the population were being drawn into politics because of the high cost of living and the food queues...the atmosphere was laden with struggle". And he says the Bolsheviks put a lot of work into explaining the causes of the crisis and agitation around the issue. So they were hardly dismissive of it as unimportant. Further, he reports that they recruited people to help with their work, because they thought the struggle around food prices was politicising the women.[40]

Somewhat contradicting their negative account of Shlyapnikov, McDermid and Hillyar comment that the Bolsheviks recognised that the increasing number of women in the metal trades, and their growing militancy, provided "some potential for agitation and organisation".

---

37. Bloodworth 2010 for a fuller account of the Bolsheviks' attitudes.
38. McDermid and Hillyar 1999, p.138.
39. Bloodworth 2013 for details of the Bolsheviks' approach.
40. Shlyapnikov 1982, pp.140, 144, 203. (McDermid and Hillyar, on p220 in footnote 53, cite p.118.)

They write: "Since at least 1915 Bolsheviks had been...addressing leaflets to both female and male workers". On IWD in 1915, the Bolsheviks had distributed a leaflet arguing "the struggle to increase wages and shorten the working day is possible only with the full participation of women workers. The task of the day is to assist in raising their class consciousness". And in one in February 1917, they note that "the appeals were gender neutral". However, they add a qualifying "although" to these observations: "[R]evolutionaries saw [the women's rising militancy] as part of the general class struggle".[41] The women's militancy *was* part of the general class struggle, fuelled by it and adding to it. The tentative "although" reflects their hesitation in accepting this key dynamic.

McDermid and Hillyar assert that the "opponents [of the tsar] ignored the evidence of female disaffection...[not] believing that it could result in more than a riot over 'bread and herrings'".[42] And they begin the chapter on women in the 1917 revolution by asserting that it was

> generally accepted by revolutionaries that women workers were incapable of sustaining either organization or industrial action, and that the cause of any female protest would be material rather than ideological, concerned with problems of everyday life rather than the wider political picture.[43]

They reference the patronising attitude of Nikolai Sukhanov, a left Menshevik and not a revolutionary, towards women clerical workers whose assessment of the coming revolution he ridiculed.[44]

The Bolsheviks based their practice on the understanding that revolutions begin, whether initiated by women or men, in much the same way as did the February Revolution. Political consciousness determined their attitude to workers, not gender; and they assumed the backward, whether male or female, could be lifted to the level of the advanced if drawn into the struggle.

---

41.   McDermid and Hillyar 1999, pp.139–41.
42.   ibid., p.140.
43.   ibid., p.143.
44.   ibid., pp.140–41.

McDermid and Hillyar assert that the Bolsheviks did not support the women going on strike on IWD because they "feared the assumed spontaneity and indiscipline of the women", only reluctantly accepting that they could not ignore the mood among them.[45] But the Bolsheviks' attitude was informed by strategic concerns about how to ensure any uprising happened when workers were ready to follow through with an assault on the regime. The small and quite passive response to the call for demonstrations on the anniversary of Bloody Sunday worried the socialists. The Bolsheviks' leading committees feared that workers were not ready for a general offensive against the regime. So they thought it better to plan for May Day, giving time to build for it. However, some of their members in the factories were for it, as was Trotsky's small group.

This would not be the last time the Bolshevik leadership would be more cautious than many of their members. On 21 June, in response to increasing agitation by many Petersburg workers and the soldiers in particular to overthrow the government, Lenin addressed them in *Pravda*. "We understand your bitterness, we understand the excitement of the Petersburg workers, but we say to them: 'Comrades, an immediate attack would be inexpedient'." And leadership bodies repeated these sentiments.[46] It is not unusual for experienced leaders of struggle to resist pressure by the less experienced for what they fear is premature action. Their rationale might well be based on an assessment of the levels of political consciousness and discipline among those pushing for action, as well as expectations of insufficient wider support or the state's response. These considerations in February were not based on gender, as McDermid and Hillyar's reference to the stereotypes about women implies, any more than they were in June.

In any case, as soon as the striking women called for support they got it, with Bolsheviks like Kayurov and other militants leading male workers out on strike, as was the tradition. But McDermid and Hillyar belittle Kayurov and other Bolsheviks' call for solidarity as motivated only by a desire to "retrieve the situation". But Kayurov wrote later, "once there is a mass strike, one must call everybody into the streets

---
45. ibid., p.147.
46. Trotsky 1977, p.521.

and take the lead". And this tradition which underpinned Bolshevism applied irrespective of gender, whether skilled or unskilled made the call. Looking for explanations of the Bolsheviks' caution in their assumed attitudes to women simply obscures vital lessons about the process of struggle.

Defying the sexist stereotypes

Revolution makes it clear that class solidarity is essential to both sides in the conflict. So among workers and the oppressed, the need for solidarity can overcome sexist divisions. Women were often able to organise and lead men, carrying out roles which challenged the sexist stereotypes.

Stites and McDermid and Hillyar have documented this process. They show the concerted and successful efforts by the Bolsheviks to involve and politically educate women. From often having to learn to read and write, these women became activists with serious responsibilities, from leading strikes and demonstrations, writing for and coordinating distribution of Bolshevik publications, to organising arms, overseeing communications and the whole tram system to ensure the insurrection in October went smoothly. The Bolshevik leadership had confidence that women, once politicised and active, could perform non-stereotypical roles.[47]

In February, two Bolshevik women organised many mass meetings and strikes including metal and tram workers, as well as helping soldiers free political prisoners. Nina Agadzhanova was on Bolshevik leadership bodies, and was elected to the Petrograd Soviet by the Vyborg district. Elena Giliarova, aged 18, served as a nurse on the Russian-Turkish war front in 1915, and as a propagandist for the Bolsheviks among the troops. After the February Revolution, she was elected by the soldiers to represent them in the Petrograd Soviet! She later played a role preparing women to fight in the Red Guards. Petronelia Zinchenko, from a poor peasant family in the Lithuania-Polish area of the empire, was working at the naval base on Kronstadt in February 1917, making sailors' uniforms. She was

---

47. Stites 1990 and McDermid and Hillyar 1999. To trace these and other women's biographies, check the index in these works.

elected to the Kronstadt Soviet and joined the Bolsheviks in August. In October she organised the sailors to go to the capital and was responsible for keeping order in the fortress and for communications between Kronstadt and Petrograd.

Arishina Kruglova helped free political prisoners in February, organised Red Guards in her area and was a delegate to two district soviets. During October, she led raids on wealthy areas, searching for arms for the Red Guards and to disarm the enemy. Serafima Zaitseva had joined the Bolsheviks aged 20 in 1915, working in metalworks. She joined the Red Guards in her factory, and was in a contingent which stormed the post office in October and fought counter-revolutionaries on the outskirts of Petrograd.

Nevertheless, assertions and hesitations sprinkled throughout *Midwives* imply the Bolsheviks were inadequate in some way, because they regarded gender issues as an integral aspect of the class struggle. But there is no other way to see the women's struggles. Take the issues workers agitated around: low and unequal pay, maternity leave, sick leave, sexual harassment at work, all issues which highlight gender oppression – and which only workers would campaign around. Bourgeois women relied on many of these conditions to ensure profits in their husband's businesses and cheap domestic labour. It was all-out class war – and only those who fought on the workers' side could seriously organise among working-class women.

Indeed Richard Stites argues that the Bolsheviks could relate to women workers much more easily than the Mensheviks because they were more radical. In their support for the government, and especially once they joined it, the Mensheviks were always compromised, wanting to send demands off to some committee to investigate, prevaricating and delaying reforms such as the eight-hour day. The Bolsheviks unequivocally supported strikes and their demands by everyone. They identified completely with the workers because they were convinced that only a second revolution in which workers took power could ensure workers' aspirations would be realised.

An important aspect of the Bolsheviks' work among women was the revival of the paper *Rabotnitsa*, banned since 1914. On its editorial board were KI Nikolaeva, PF Kudelli, KN Samoilova,

Elizarova, Bonch-Bruevich, Kollontai, and Ludmilla Stahl – stalwarts of women's liberation, and leading Bolsheviks for many years. An editorial board which included factory representatives met weekly to review the reports received from the different areas. Published twice monthly, it reached a circulation of about 50,000. It dealt with political questions of the war, critiquing the Provisional Government, and with economic grievances, as well as explaining the Bolshevik position on women's oppression.

The Bolsheviks used *Rabotnitsa* to agitate among and organise women workers and soldiers' wives. As women's strikes, like one by 8,000 laundresses in May, grew in number and militancy, they mobilised support. They staged huge political meetings that often spilled out of the hall into the street. On 11 June 10,000 turned up at the Cinzinelli Circus to hear speeches on the topic of "The War and High Prices". The paper also addressed male workers, arguing for them to see women as an integral part of the workers' movement. McDermid and Hillyar give a good outline of the approach:

> [O]n the one hand this entailed challenging the stereotype of the passive, conservative woman and insisting on the principle of sexual equality. On the other hand, it focused on "women's" issues (such as crèches, nurseries, maternity benefits and protective labour legislation), as well as those "domestic" problems associated with the war.[48]

They document that the Bolshevik Party fought to have women represented on factory committees in industries where they constituted a significant portion of the workforce (notably textiles), which involved persuading men to vote for them.[49] And they fought the prevalent idea that with growing unemployment, men should get priority over women, especially using their influence in the metalworkers' union.

And yet, in their conclusion McDermid and Hillyar express the classic putdown of women in their effort to limit the achievements of the Bolsheviks: "These 'midwives of the revolution' were poorly educated and drawn to simple explanations for their plight". It was

---
48. McDermid and Hillyar 1999, pp.165–66.
49. ibid., p.166.

hardly a "simple" matter to come to understand that only a new revolution would realise their demands and that the only organisation committed to those demands was the Bolsheviks. However, as if they realise, mid-sentence, how insulting that is towards women who played a role in a revolution, they conclude:

> [B]ut they were not simply blank pages on which the Bolsheviks could write. Rather, they eventually turned to the Bolshevik Party because it alone seemed to articulate their concerns as women and as workers, and to appreciate that they wanted these addressed as a matter of urgency.[50]

McDermid and Hillyar refer to the "narrowness" and "limited in practice" features of Bolshevik work – without ever suggesting what wider or less limited practices would have consisted of. But on the other hand, they say that the Bolsheviks "seem to have been influenced more by class than gender", and so "the women didn't challenge their gender roles but tended to justify their activities with reference to their traditional domestic responsibilities".[51] So in the contradictory world of identity politics and suspicion of class as a basis on which to analyse women's oppression, at one minute they erroneously assert that the Bolsheviks didn't campaign around specific gender issues. But when forced to admit they did, it is another negative as it reinforced the sexist stereotypes.

Much has been written about the role of the prominent leading Bolshevik women, such as Krupskaya, Inessa Armand, Alexandra Kollontai and many others, not always accurately, reducing them to Lenin's wife or lover, or inappropriately labelled a "feminist" rather than a Marxist revolutionary. These women were in the main from the educated middle and upper classes, as were most leading male socialists. Their privileged position made it possible to be involved when working-class women were quiescent, held down by poverty and appalling oppression. But there can be no doubt about the serious attitude of the Bolsheviks towards working-class women once they moved out of the shadows.

---

50. ibid., p.200.
51. ibid., pp.200–201.

Women were about 10 percent of the Bolshevik membership in 1917, and in the party and among workers, women often had responsibilities regarded as more appropriate for women, things like secretarial and organisational roles, rather than theoretical writing, etc. But we need to think of the context: high levels of illiteracy and little education for women generally. Many of the women who became Bolsheviks first had to learn to read and write. Contraception was difficult and unreliable, maternal support virtually non-existent, and limited legal rights hardly encouraged women to live independently from men. The historian Ralph Carter Elwood, writing about women revolutionaries in the Ukraine, makes some insightful points. He insists on the importance of what is often just dismissed as unimportant, "humdrum" (in the words of one historian) secretarial jobs, and argues that these were vital roles, involving political judgement. Women were often responsible for coding of messages, arranging secret addresses, serving as liaison between illegal and legal outlets. And he concludes:

> We need to stop condescending to these "daughters" and "brides" [we could add "midwives"] of the revolution, who possessed courage as well as dedication, initiative as well as selflessness. The achievements of Marxist women in Russia have to be set within the context of a very limited range of options open to women in such a patriarchal society.[52]

Conclusion

The issues at stake are not just historical. They are alive in the struggles of today. Clearly women played less of a leading role because of the structural oppression they suffered. But talk of political leadership as a "male hierarchy" of the movement is drastically disorienting. In mass struggle, the most advanced, class conscious and organised need to lead if any gains are to be won. Opposition to them taking the lead on the basis of their gender or any other identity would be nothing but counterproductive.

---

52. Elwood 1974, pp.67–68.

Wade argues that socialists "rejected a separate feminist agenda as a distraction from the main struggle".⁵³ This is argued today about Marxists. Then and now it misstates the issue. How could there have been a "separate feminist agenda" to which working women were committed? The Mensheviks and Socialist Revolutionaries and the feminist movement to which they subscribed, like the Bolsheviks, had a class agenda, not a "separate feminist" one. But theirs was that of the capitalist class, whose rule could only maintain women's oppression.

The Bolsheviks argued that the economic, social and structural changes necessary to achieve women's liberation would only be possible after a further, workers' revolution. But it is absolutely clear from the histories written by Wade, McDermid and Hillyar and Stites, that the Bolsheviks did not ignore women's rights before that revolution. Like all revolutionary Marxists, they understood that for successful workers' struggles of any magnitude, workers need to be involved in fighting for the rights of the oppressed in their ranks. And the oppressed need to be drawn into that struggle.

The October Revolution created a workers' state. Tragically it was destroyed. The defeat of the workers' revolutions which swept Europe, and counter-revolution backed up by imperialist invasions by the supposedly enlightened Allied powers, destroyed the workers' democracy along with the economy. This laid the basis for Stalin's rule, under which all the gains of women, workers and peasants, were rolled back.⁵⁴ Nevertheless, the workers' state in Russia took humanity the closest we have ever been to socialism, and therefore to women's liberation.

It was only after the October insurrection that the Bolsheviks could begin to lay the basis for a society with different attitudes to gender. It involved trying to establish a whole different framework, both ideologically and in terms of infrastructure – things like communal eating and state-run childcare, challenging the age-old patriarchal structures of the family.⁵⁵

---

53. Wade 2000, pp.117–18.
54. For an explanation of this process of counter-revolution see Arnove et al. 2003.
55. A discussion of those achievements is beyond the scope of this article. See Bloodworth 2010.

Any revolution will rupture society along class lines. So defensiveness about the centrality of class and concessions to identity politics can only be a distraction from the struggle for a workers' movement which can lead a revolution again.

The class divisions among women have not been eliminated by improvements in women's lives. Ruling class women now have their own businesses and so directly benefit from the oppressive conditions of working-class women in the form of profits. And their exploitative position is strengthened by the divisions caused by sexism which undermine a united workers' struggle. So they will no more support our demands than they did one hundred years ago. Hillary Clinton, Julia Gillard, Theresa May, Angela Merkel and Gina Rinehart are only some of the better known, but they graphically illustrate the point.

Stites concludes: "[I]t is clear that the Bolsheviks never had any real competition as organizers and propagandists among women of the urban lower classes in 1917".[56] This testimony confirms that the revolutionary, class orientation of the Bolsheviks made them the most effective organisers in the fight for women's liberation. It matters that we draw the correct lessons from their experience, the better to understand how to lead such a fight for human liberation again.

References

Arnove, Anthony, Peter Binns, Tony Cliff, Chris Harman, Ahmed Shawki 2003, *Russia: From Workers' State to State Capitalism*, Haymarket Books.

Barker, Colin (ed.) 2002 [1987], *Revolutionary Rehearsals*, Haymarket Books.

Bloodworth, Sandra 2010, "Marx and Engels on Women's and Sexual Oppression and their Legacy", *Marxist Left Review*, 1, Spring. https://marxistleftreview.org/articles/marx-and-engels-on-womens-and-sexual-oppression-and-their-legacy/

Bloodworth, Sandra 2013, "Lenin vs 'Leninism'", *Marxist Left Review*, 5, Summer. https://marxistleftreview.org/articles/lenin-vs-leninism/

---

56. Stites 1990, p.300.

Cliff, Tony 2004 [1976], *All Power to the Soviets. Lenin 1914-1917*, Haymarket Books.

Donald, Moira 1982, "Bolshevik activity amongst the working women of Petrograd in 1917", *International Review of Social History*, 27 (2).

Elwood, Ralph Carter 1974, *Russian Social Democracy in the Underground: A Study of the RSDLP in the Ukraine, 1907–1914*, Assen.

Harman, Chris 1988, *Class Struggles in Eastern Europe 1945–83*, Bookmarks.

Harris, Carolyn 2017, "Russia's February Revolution Was Led by Women on the March", Smithsonian.com.

Mandel, David 1983, *The Petrograd Workers and the Fall of the Old Regime. From the February Revolution to the July Days 1917*, St Martin's Press.

McDermid, Jane and Anna Hillyar 1999, *Midwives of the Revolution: Female Bolsheviks and Women Workers in 1917*, UCL Press.

Shlyapnikov, Alexander 1982, *On the eve of 1917. Reminiscences from the Revolutionary Underground*, Allison and Busby.

Smith, Steve A 1983, *Red Petrograd. Revolution in the factories 1917–1918*, Cambridge University Press.

Smith, Steve A 1987, "Petrograd in 1917: the view from below", in Daniel Kaiser (ed.), *The Workers' Revolution in Russia, 1917. The View from Below*, Cambridge University Press.

Sorokin, Pitirim 1950, *Leaves from a Russian Diary*, The Beacon Press.

Stites, Richard 1990, *The Women's Liberation Movement in Russia. Feminism, Nihilism and Bolshevism, 1860-1930*, Princeton University Press.

Trotsky, Leon 1977 [1930], *The History of the Russian Revolution*, Pluto Press.

Wade, Rex A 2000, *The Russian Revolution, 1917*, Cambridge University Press.

Glossary

1. People

Chernov: A leader of the Socialist Revolutionaries, standing between the Rights and the Lefts. Minister for agriculture in the coalition government.

Denikin: Tsarist general. Commanded anti-Bolshevik forces in southern Russia after 1917.

Kamenev: Member of the Central Committee of the Bolsheviks; publicly opposed the October Revolution.

Kerensky: A Socialist Revolutionary in 1917 (previously a Trudovik in the Duma). First minister of justice, then of war and marine, and finally "minister-president" of the provisional government. Fled from Russia after the October Revolution.

Kornilov: Russian general in command of the Petrograd district from the first days of the February Revolution. Tried to establish a military dictatorship late August 1917.

Lenin: Leader of the Bolsheviks, an active revolutionary since 1887, joined Plekhanov's Marxist study circles in 1893. Returned to Russia in April 1917 from exile in Switzerland in a "sealed train" by agreement with the German government. First head of the Soviet government. Died in January 1924 partly from wounds inflicted in an assassination attempt on 30 August 1918 by Fanny Kaplan, a Socialist Revolutionary.

Prince Lvov: A Cadet (Constitutional Democrat), first prime minister after the February Revolution.

Martov: The ideological leader of the Mensheviks and an irreconcilable opponent of the Soviet government. Emigrated to Berlin in 1923.

Miliukov (sometimes spelt Milyukov): Head of the Cadets (Constitutional Democrats), minister of foreign affairs and actual boss of the provisional government.

Plekhanov: Regarded as the "father of Russian Marxism" because he pioneered Marxist discussion circles in the 1880s; translator of Marx. Moved to the right after the 1905 revolution. Took a patriotic position on the war and was a right-wing socialist during 1917.

Stalin: Member of the Central Committee of the Bolsheviks, editor with Kamenev of their paper *Pravda*, until Lenin's arrival in Russia in April 1917. General Secretary of the party 1922. Led the counter-revolution from 1924 and remained head of the bureaucratic government until his death in 1953.

Sukhanov: A moderate socialist, belonged to a group organised by the novelist Maxim Gorky. One of the leaders of the Petrograd Soviet Executive Committee after February. Author of memoirs published as *The Russian Revolution 1917. A Personal Record*.

Trotsky: One of the most loved orators of the revolutionary movement. Active from the years 1896–97 and elected President of the Petrograd Soviet at the age of 26. Joined the Bolsheviks in July 1917 and became one of its two principle leaders beside Lenin. Trotsky developed the theory of permanent revolution which Lenin adopted in its fundamentals in his *April Theses*. From 1913 Trotsky led his own organisation, the Mezhraiontsy, which remained independent of both the Bolsheviks and

Mensheviks. Played a leading role in Petrograd once he reached Russia in May 1917. Author of the magnificent epic *History of the Russian Revolution*, the best account of the revolutionary year. Expelled from the Communist Party of the Soviet Union in 1927 and exiled in 1929. Never ceased to campaign against Stalin's bureaucratic rule and to keep alive the genuine traditions of Marxism and Bolshevism. Murdered by a Stalinist agent in 1940 in his home in Mexico.

Tsereteli (sometimes spelt Tseretelli): Leader of the Mensheviks and principal leader of the Soviet until the Bolsheviks won a majority.

Zinoviev: Member of the Central Committee of the Bolsheviks. Came to Russia with Lenin on the sealed train in April from Switzerland. Publicly opposed the October insurrection. First president of the Third (Communist) International, or Comintern, in 1919.

2. Political parties and organisations

Cadets (sometimes spelt Kadets): Popular name for the Constitutional Democrats; the great liberal party favouring a constitutional monarchy, or ultimately a republic. The party of the progressive landlords, middle bourgeoisie and bourgeois intelligentsia, headed by Miliukov, a professor of history.

Mensheviks: Moderate socialist party who claimed to be Marxist, but advocated that the working class combine with the liberal bourgeoisie to overthrow the monarchy and establish a democratic republic. The result of a split in the Social Democratic Party in 1903. The other faction out of the split was Lenin's Bolsheviks.

Socialist Revolutionaries (Trotsky refers to them as Social Revolutionaries in his *History*): Peasant socialist party. A populist party which represented the wavering interests of the small peasants in the revolution. It split between the Right who supported Kerensky and the Left Socialist Revolutionaries, who were semi-anarchist in their leanings. The Left SRs participated in the Bolshevik government until the Brest-Litovsk peace agreement, which they opposed, was signed with Germany in March 1918.

Notes

Preface

1. For an introduction to the Marxist method see Paul D'Amato, *The Meaning of Marxism*, Haymarket Books, Chicago, 2007.
2. See Chris Harman, *Class Struggles in Eastern Europe 1945-83*, Bookmarks, London, 1988 for how those states were set up.
3. Tony Cliff, *State Capitalism in Russia*, Bookmarks, London, 1988 (first published as *Stalinist Russia: A Marxist Analysis*, 1955); Anthony Arnove, Peter Binns, Tony Cliff, Chris Harman, Ahmed Shawki, *Russia: From Workers' State to State Capitalism*, Haymarket Books, Chicago, 2003. For a summary of the interpretations that have dominated histories of the revolution see Edward Acton, "The Revolution and its Historians" in *Critical Companion to the Russian Revolution 1914-1921*, Arnold, London, 1997. A more recent historiography by a Marxist is Kevin Murphy, "Can we write the history of the Russian Revolution? A Defense of the Bolshevik Revolution" in *International Socialist Review* 57, Jan-Feb 2008.
4. Leon Trotsky, *The Permanent Revolution & Results and Prospects*, Pathfinder Press, New York, 1969 or available at www.marxists.org. Trotsky's theory of permanent revolution was a break from the orthodox Marxist position that the coming revolution would be a bourgeois democratic one and the capitalist class would come to power in a republic. Then workers would have to fight for socialism. Lenin essentially adopted Trotsky's position in April 1917 in his *April Theses*.
5. Edward Acton, "The Revolution and its Historians", p. 5.
6. A very accessible volume that brings together a range of these authors is Daniel H Kaiser (ed), *The Workers' Revolution in Russia 1917. The View from Below*, Cambridge University Press, 1987.
7. Richard Pipes, *Russian Revolution*, Fontana, 1992; Orlando Figes, *People's Tragedy. The Russian Revolution 1891-1924*, Pimlico, 1996.
8. Edward Acton, "The Revolution and its Historians", p. 13.
9. Orlando Figes, *People's Tragedy*, p. 484.

Introduction

10. Pitirim Sorokin, *Leaves from a Russian Diary*, The Beacon Press, Boston, 1950, p. 3.
11. Richard Stites, *The Women's Liberation Movement in Russia. Feminism, Nihilism and Bolshevism, 1860-1930*, Princeton University Press, Princeton New Jersey, 1990, p. 290.
12. See Sandra Bloodworth (ed), *Workers' Revolutions of the Twentieth Century*, Socialist Alternative pamphlet.

Chapter one – The February Revolution

13. Steve A Smith, "Petrograd in 1917: the view from below" in Daniel Kaiser (ed), *The View from Below*, p. 61.
14. Rex Wade, *The Russian Revolution, 1917*, Cambridge University Press, Cambridge, 2000, p. 31.
15. Leon Trotsky, *The History of the Russian Revolution*, Pluto Press, London, 1977, p. 121. Also available at www.marxists.org. See chapter VII, "Five Days (23-27 February 1917)".

16. Rex Wade, *The Russian Revolution, 1917*, pp. 33-34.
17. Trotsky, *History*, pp. 124-125.
18. Trotsky, *History*, p. 129, chapter VII "Five Days".
19. A Tyrkova-Williams, *From Liberty to Brest-Litovsk*, Macmillan, London, 1919, pp. 4, 10-11.
20. Trotsky, *History*, pp. 46-47.
21. Rex Wade, *The Russian Revolution, 1917*, p. 29.
22. Richard Stites, *The Women's Liberation Movement in Russia*, pp. 288-289.
23. Quoted in *Socialist Worker* (US), 2 March, 2007 at www.socialistworker.org/2007-1/621/621_08_February.shtml.
24. Richard Stites, *The Women's Liberation Movement in Russia*, p. 290.
25. Rex Wade, *The Russian Revolution, 1917*, p. 32.
26. Rex Wade, *The Russian Revolution, 1917*, p. 37.
27. Rex Wade, *The Russian Revolution, 1917*, p. 32.
28. Trotsky, *History*, pp. 169-171.

Chapter two – The impact of the February Revolution

29. WH Chamberlain, *The Russian Revolution, vol. 1, 1917-1918, from the Overthrow of the Tsar to the Assumption of Power by the Bolsheviks*, Princeton, 1987.
30. Steve A Smith, "Petrograd in 1917: the view from below", p. 62.
31. Trotsky, *History*, p. 157.
32. Rex Wade, *The Russian Revolution, 1917*, p. 90.
33. For a good account of the factory committees see SA Smith, *Red Petrograd. Revolution in the factories 1917-1918*, Cambridge University Press, London, 1983.
34. Quoted in Mike Haynes, "Was There a Parliamentary Alternative in 1917?" in *International Socialism* no 76, Autumn 1997, London, p. 13. Also available at www.isj.org.uk.
35. Morgan Philips Price, *Dispatches from the Revolution Russia 1916-1918*, Pluto Press, London, 1997, p. 60.
36. Steven A Smith, *Red Petrograd*; Rex Wade, *The Russian Revolution, 1917*, pp. 89-100.
37. Rex A Wade, *The Russian Revolution, 1917*.
38. John Reed, *Ten Days That Shook the World*, Sutton Publishing, illustrated edition, 1997, p. 21.
39. Richard Stites, *The Women's Liberation Movement in Russia*, p. 295.
40. Morgan Philips Price, *Dispatches*, p. 30.
41. Morgan Philips Price, *Dispatches*, pp. 31-32.

Chapter three – February: the unfinished revolution

42. Morgan Philips Price, *Dispatches*, p. 30.
43. See Sandra Bloodworth (ed), *Workers' Revolutions of the Twentieth Century*; and Trotsky, *History*, Chapter 11, "Dual Power".
44. Trotsky, *History*. This quote and following one pp. 201-211.
45. Trotsky, *History*, p. 213.
46. Rex A Wade, *The Russian Revolution, 1917*, p. 91.
47. SA Smith, "Petrograd in 1917", p. 62.
48. Trotsky, *History*, p. 217.
49. NN Sukhanov, *The Russian Revolution 1917. A Personal Record*, Princeton University Press, Princeton, 1984, p. 167.
50. Quoted in Trotsky, *History*, p. 692.
51. Trotsky, *History*, p. 178.
52. Trotsky, *History*, pp. 183-184.
53. Trotsky, *History*, p. 178.
54. Trotsky, *History*, p. 217.
55. Trotsky, *History*, p. 221.
56. NN Sukhanov, *The Russian Revolution*, pp. 273-274.
57. Quoted in Trotsky, *History* pp. 313-314.
58. Lenin, *Collected Works* vol. 24, p. 146.
59. Trotsky, *History*, p. 342.

60. Quoted in Tony Cliff, *All Power to the Soviets. Lenin 1914-1917*, Haymarket Books, Chicago, 2004, p. 170.
61. Trotsky, *History*, p. 347.
62. Trotsky, *History*, p. 347.
63. NN Sukhanov, *The Russian Revolution 1917*, p. 317.
64. Trotsky, *History*, p. 359.
65. Trotsky, *History*, p. 359.

Chapter four – The struggle for October

66. Kerensky and Browder (eds), *The Russian Provisional Government 1917 Documents* vol. III, Stanford University Press, Ca, p. 1282.
67. Quoted in Cliff, *All Power to the Soviets*, p. 177.
68. Quoted in Cliff, *All Power to the Soviets*, p. 182.
69. Alexander Rabinowitch, *Prelude to Revolution. The Petrograd Bolsheviks and the July 1917 Uprising*, Indiana University Press, Bloomington, 1968, p. 106.
70. NN Sukhanov, *The Russian Revolution*, pp. 416-417.
71. Alexander Rabinowitch, *Prelude to Revolution*, p. 148.
72. Tony Cliff, *All Power to the Soviets*, chapter 14.
73. Alexander Rabinowitch, *Prelude to Revolution*, this and following quotes, pp. 121-122.
74. Orlando Figes, in his *People's Tragedy*, pp. 425-427, sums up the evidence and rejects Pipe's account. His way of denigrating the Bolsheviks is to emphasise how confused they were, and that Lenin was "hopelessly paralysed by indecision" with no political understanding of the dangers Lenin knew confronted them.
75. Margot Morcombe and Mark Fielding, *The Spirit of Change. Russia in Revolution*, McGraw-Hill, Sydney, 1998, p. 122. For Lenin's arguments, see his *Collected Works*, vol. 25.
76. Trotsky, *History*, p. 430.
77. Trotsky, *History*, and following quote, pp. 457-458.
78. Kerensky and Browder, p. 1261.
79. Kerensky and Browder (eds), *Documents*, vol. III, this and next quotation, p. 731-732.
80. John Reed, *Ten Days That Shook the World*, International Publishers, New York, 1934, pp. 7-8.
81. Kerensky and Browder, vol. II, p. 723.
82. Kerensky and Browder, vol. II, p. 750.
83. Kerensky and Browder, p. 1527, quoted in document 1260, "The Recollection of AI Putilov".
84. John Reed, *Ten Days*, p. 27.
85. John Reed, *Ten Days*, p. 8.
86. Tony Cliff, *All Power to the Soviets*, pp. 287-288.
87. Lenin, *Collected Works*, vol. 25, pp. 285-289 for this quote and more of Lenin's writing on the coup.
88. NN Sukhanov, *The Russian Revolution*, p. 505.
89. David Mandel, *The Petrograd Workers and the Soviet Seizure of Power*, quoted in Derek Howl, "Bookwatch: The Russian Revolution" in *International Socialism* no 62, Spring 1994, London, p. 140. Available at www.isj.org.uk.
90. Trotsky, *History*, p. 736.
91. Tony Cliff, *All Power to the Soviets*, p. 297.
92. Lenin, "Social-Chauvinist Policy Behind a Cover of Internationalist Phrases", written in 1915 about the crisis caused by the war, *Collected Works*, vol. 21, p. 429.

Chapter five – October: the workers take power

93. Lenin, *Collected Works*, vol. 26, p. 24.
94. Lenin, *Collected Works*, vol. 26, pp. 22-23. Trotsky would sum up these arguments and draw out the lessons of October after the revolution in *The Lessons of October*, available from Red Flag Books.
95. Orlando Figes, The *People's Tragedy*, p. 484.
96. NN Sukhanov, *The Russian Revolution*, p. 523.
97. Lenin, *Collected Works*, vol. 26, pp. 48-50.

98. Morcombe and Fielding, *The Spirit of Change*, p. 130.
99. Chris Corin and Terry Fiehn, *Communist Russia under Lenin and Stalin*, The Schools History Project official text, (no date), pp. 49–58.
100. Alexander Rabinowitch, *The Bolsheviks Come to Power. The Revolution of 1917 in Petrograd*, Haymarket Books, Chicago, 2004 (first published 1976).
101. Rabinowitch, *The Bolsheviks Come to Power*, this quote and the following account pp. 227–232.
102. Rabinowitch, *The Bolsheviks Come to Power*, p. 214.
103. Orlando Figes, *People's Tragedy*, pp. 480–484.
104. Rabinowitch, *The Bolsheviks Come to Power*, pp. 239–243.
105. Rabinowitch, *The Bolsheviks Come to Power*, pp. 245–246.
106. Trotsky, *History*, p. 1034.
107. Trotsky, *History*, pp. 1038-1039. Rex Wade, in *The Russian Revolution, 1917* gives an account of the mobilisation before 25 October, pp. 227–239.
108. Trotsky, *History*, p. 1124.
109. Trotsky, *History*, pp. 1066–1067.
110. Trotsky, *History*, pp. 1054–1055 and p. 1068.
111. Trotsky, *History*, pp. 1078–1079.
112. Quoted in Tony Cliff, *Revolution Besieged. Lenin 1917-1923*, Pluto Press, London, 1978, p. 2.
113. From a letter from Martov to Axelrod, his collaborator, days after the insurrection. Quoted in Tony Cliff, The *Revolution Besieged*, p. 2.

Chapter six – The Bolsheviks and the masses

114. Quoted in Steve Smith, "Petrograd in 1917" in Daniel H Kaiser, *The View from Below*, p. 73.
115. Lenin, "Can the Bolsheviks Retain State Power?" in *Collected Works*, vol. 26, pp. 87–136.
116. Steve A Smith, "Petrograd 1917" in Daniel H Kaiser, *The View from Below*, p. 77.
117. Diane P Koenker, "Moscow in 1917:the view from below" in Daniel Kaiser (ed) *The View from Below*, p. 91.
118. Trotsky, *History*, this and following quotes, pp. 760–766.
119. Trotsky, *History*, p. 768.
120. Trotsky, *History*, p. 736.
121. Trotsky, *History*, this quote and the following points, pp. 1147–1148.
122. Morgan Philips Price, *Dispatches*, p. 88.
123. Trotsky, *History*, p. 788.
124. Trotsky, *History*, p. 809.
125. Lenin, *Collected Works*, vol. 25, p. 130.
126. Lenin, *Collected Works*, vol. 25, p. 133.
127. Trotsky, *History*, p. 809.
128. Trotsky, *History*, p. 810.
129. Quoted in Steve A Smith, "Petrograd in 1917", in Daniel H Kaiser, *The View from Below*, p. 77.
130. Trotsky, *History*, p. 1029.

Chapter seven – After October

131. A Rabinowitch, *The Bolsheviks Come to Power*, pp. 274–275.
132. John Reed, *Ten Days*.
133. These articles have been published in various editions and are available at www.marxists.org.
134. I Deutscher (ed), *The Age of Permanent Revolution: A Trotsky Anthology*, New York, 1964, p. 301.
135. Richard Stites, *The Women's Liberation Movement in Russia*, p. 264.
136. Dan Healey, *Homosexual Desire in Revolutionary Russia. The Regulation of Sexual and Gender Dissent*, University of Chicago Press, Chicago, 2001, p. 111.

Chapter eight – The first step in the international socialist revolution

137. Trotsky, *History*, pp. 1184–1185.
138. Tony Cliff, *State Capitalism in Russia*, Bookmarks; for a summary of the arguments see Anthony Arnove et al, *Russia: From Workers' State to State Capitalism*. Leon Trotsky, *The Revolution Betrayed* available in various editions, available at www.marxists.org.
139. Tony Cliff, *State Capitalism in Russia*, pp. 46–47.
140. Chris Harman, "The nature of Stalinist Russia and the Eastern Bloc" in Anthony Arnove et al *Russia: From Workers' State to State Capitalism*, p. 48.
141. Michael Reiman, *The Birth of Stalinism. The USSR on the Eve of the "Second Revolution"*, Indiana University Press, Indianapolis, 1987, p. 13.
142. Quoted in RW Davies, *The Soviet Economy in Turmoil, 1929–1930*, MacMillan, Basingstoke, 1989, p. 442.
143. Lenin *Collected Works*, vol. 24, p. 513.
144. Maurice Brinton, *The Bolsheviks & Workers' Control 1917 to 1921. The State and Counter-Revolution*, Solidarity, London, 1970.
145. Diane Koenker, "Moscow in 1917" in Daniel Kaiser (ed), *The View from Below*, p. 97.
146. This and following quote in Chris Harman, "The nature of Stalinist Russia" in Anthony Arnove et al, *From Workers' State to State Capitalism*, pp. 39–40.
147. For a summary of the conditions and the Bolsheviks' response see Tony Cliff, *Revolution Besieged. Lenin 1917–1923*, Pluto Press, London, 1978, especially chapters 6 and 7, pp. 66–98.
148. Duncan Hallas, *The Comintern*, Haymarket Books, Chicago, 2008; available at www.marxists.org.
149. Lenin, *Collected Works*, vol. 32, p. 169.
150. Daniel Lopez and Corey Oakley, "New facts explode anarchist myth" in *Socialist Alternative*, no. 100, March 2006, available at www.sa.org.au. Original source at www.marxist.com/History/Trotsky_was_right.html.
151. Lenin, *Collected Works*, vol. 32, p. 215.
152. Michael Reiman, *The Birth of Stalinism*, p. 22. All the information on the United Opposition in 1927 is from Reiman, chapter three, "The Opposition Revived".
153. Tony Cliff, *Trotsky. Fighting the rising Stalinist bureaucracy 1923–1927*, Bookmarks, London, 1991, p. 277.
154. Tony Cliff, *Trotsky 1923–27*, p. 249.
155. Tony Cliff, *Trotsky 1923–27*, p. 279.
156. Duncan Hallas, *The Comintern*.
157. Trotsky, *History*, Appendix II "Socialism in a Separate Country?", pp. 1219–1257. This "theory" has also been central to the ruling ideology of all the one-party dictatorships that have called themselves "Communist", from Eastern Europe to China, Cuba and some African states. None of them were created by workers' revolutions, making it even clearer, if proof were needed, that this kind of state had nothing to do with the traditions of Marxism and the self-emancipation of the working class.
158. Liz Walsh, "The Gulag Trotskyists" in *Socialist Alternative*, no. 124, January 2008. Available at www.sa.org.au.
159. Biographies of Trotsky include a four volume biography by Tony Cliff published by Bookmarks, London, and a three volume biography by Isaac Deutscher. The most accessible account of Trotsky's ideas is Duncan Hallas, *Trotsky's Marxism and other essays*, Haymarket Books, Chicago, 2003. Trotsky's writings are available at www.marxists.org.

Chapter nine – Was there a more peaceful, parliamentary road?

160. Quoted in Kevin Murphy, "A Defense of the Bolshevik Revolution", pp. 48–49. Available at www.isreview.org.
161. Victor Serge, *Year One of the Russian Revolution*, Pluto Press and Bookmarks, London, 1992, p. 75.
162. Serge, *Year One*, p. 187–188.
163. Boris Ivanovich Kolonitskii, "'Democracy' in the Political Consciousness of the February

Revolution" in Rex A Wade (ed), *Revolutionary Russia. New Approaches*, Routledge, New York, 2004, p. 78.
164. Serge, *Year One*, pp. 188-189.
165. A Rabinowitch, *The Bolsheviks Come to Power*, p. 296.
166. PA Milyukov, *History of the Second Russian Revolution*, quoted in Morcombe and Fielding, *The Spirit of Change*, p. 139.
167. Trotsky, *History*, p. 713.
168. Trotsky, *History*, p. 738.
169. Trotsky, *History*, p. 173.
170. John Reed, *Ten Days*, p. 7.
171. Trotsky, *History*, p. 715.
172. Trotsky, *History*, p. 1181.
173. Mike Haynes, "Was there a parliamentary alternative in Russia 1917?" All quotes from pp. 56-57. Alexander Rabinowitch agrees with this assessment in *The Bolsheviks Come to Power*, quoted in Kevin Murphy, "A Defense of the October Revolution". Victor Serge gives the same assessment of who was to blame for the failure to form a coalition government in *Year One*, p. 83.
174. Trotsky, *History*, pp. 1152-1153.
175. Trotsky, *History*, p. 1183.
176. Rex Wade, *The Russian Revolution, 1917*, p. 297.
177. Victor Serge, *Year One*, p. 126.
178. Quoted in Pierre Broué, *The German Revolution 1917-1923*, Haymarket Books, Chicago, 2006, p. 166.
179. Victor Serge, *Year One*, p. 130.
180. Kevin Murphy, "A Defense of the October Revolution", pp. 48-49. The study of Saratov is Donald Raleigh, *Experiencing Russia's Civil War Politics, Society and Revolutionary Culture in Saratov, 1917-1922*, Princeton University Press, 2002.
181. Victor Serge, *Year One*, pp. 134-135.
182. Pierre Broué, *The German Revolution 1917-1923*, Chapter 9, "The period of dual power", pp. 157-188.
183. Pierre Broué, *The German Revolution 1917-1923*.
184. Pierre Broué, *The German Revolution 1917-1923*, p. 168.

Chapter ten – The relevance of 1917 for today

185. Pierre Broué, *The German Revolution 1917-1923*, p. 116.
186. Megan Trudell, "The Russian civil war: a Marxist analysis" in *International Socialism*, 86, Spring 2000. Available at www.isj.org.uk.
187. Pierre Broué, *The German Revolution 1917-1923*, p. 167. Chris Harman, *The Lost Revolution Germany 1918-1923*, Bookmarks, London, 1982 also deals with these arguments.

Further reading

Leon Trotsky, *The History of the Russian Revolution*, Pluto Press, London, 1977. Also available at www.marxists.org.

Alexander Rabinowitch, *Prelude to Revolution. The Petrograd Bolsheviks and the July 1917 Uprising*, Indiana University Press, Bloomington, 1968.

Tony Cliff, *All Power to the Soviets. Lenin 1914-1917*, Red Flag Books, Melbourne, 2023.

Daniel H Kaiser (ed), *The Workers' Revolution in Russia 1917. The View from Below*, Cambridge University Press, 1987.

This work was published by Red Flag Books, an imprint of the revolutionary organisation Socialist Alternative.

Red Flag Books offers hundreds of other titles covering Marxist politics, revolutionary history, and more.

Browse our store at *shop.redflag.org.au*

—

Read on to discover other important projects that help to equip us with the ideas we need to fight back and win against capitalism.

REDFLAG

the newspaper of Socialist Alternative

Australia has one of the world's most concentrated mainstream media landscapes.

We produce Red Flag to provide an anticapitalist voice in Australian politics.

We also want to provide an educational resource: we cover the hidden history of class struggle and the core concepts in Marxist theory.

We raise awareness of international struggles, and we try to make a contribution to international debates on the socialist left.

To continue publication, we need the backing of readers.

Get a subscription at **subscribe.redflag.org.au** to support our project, and even receive exclusive content and offers as thanks.

www.ingramcontent.com/pod-product-compliance
Lightning Source LLC
Chambersburg PA
CBHW012005090526
44590CB00026B/3876